The 6 STEPS 2 ONLINE BUSINESS SUCCESS

You Can't FAIL if You Don't Quit

Pat Headley

Contents

Preface 1

Chapter 1
Desire 5

Chapter 2
Motivation 19

Chapter 3
Planning/goal-setting 43

Chapter 4
Coachability 63

Chapter 5
Attitude 79

Chapter 6
Commitment 93

Chapter 7
Conclusion: the future of internet marketing 107

Preface

Why I wrote this book

After making a strategy shift to focus my business activities online, it quickly became apparent that many who look to the Internet as a means of developing a business were failing at the first hurdle. I recognized that this was not due to a lack of product-specific knowledge but something more generic, a thread that ran through all successful business people, and a fundamental component of success in whatever their chosen field — their own personal development.

This led me to examine my own background, given the many setbacks I have encountered on my own path. I could have chosen to sit comfortably in my armchair in front of the TV, instead of making the choice to pursue my dream – a dream that led me to attain more success in business than I had ever experienced and gave me the opportunity to contribute to the charitable causes that are dear to me, and to which I donate the proceeds of this book.

I write this book in the hope that those who decide to pursue an online business will understand what is required to become successful. I pull no punches; I tell it like it is. The book will also be a valuable guide for anyone wishing to start a traditional bricks-and-mortar business, as the principles for success are generic.

For those whose dreams of online success have faded, it is my hope that this will inspire you to rise and to achieve the success you justly deserve. The online world is still in its infancy and there is a world of opportunity waiting for those who are willing to pursue an ethical and professional online business.

What is an entrepreneur?

I believe that many of us are more entrepreneurial than we choose to give ourselves credit for. What is the picture that forms in your mind when you hear the word 'entrepreneur'. Is it that of someone who is successful? Someone who takes risks? Someone who has defied the odds and overcome challenges to achieve success? The fact is, we all have these traits. I

Preface

believe it's an inborn human instinct. If we look into our childhood days we will recognize things we did that give evidence of this.

When I look back over my early teens, growing up as a young man in what some would call a deprived part of London, I recall opening a cycle repair business. This would entail regular visits to the local refuse dump to salvage broken cycle parts, an exercise that was not without its dangers and was sometimes fun, playing cat and mouse with the security guard at the dump. As you can imagine, it was not a safe place for children.

On a Saturday afternoon many of the local kids would line up with their cycles outside my parents' house where I had a workshop in the basement. I would spend most of the weekend repairing cycles and selling my salvaged cycle parts to the local kids. At the time I don't think I had heard of the word entrepreneur, let alone know what one was.

As I advanced into my late teens I studied electronics at my local college which led me to embark on a TV repair business. I remember living with my girlfriend at the time and turning our living room into a TV repair workshop. Funnily enough I remember being brought every conceivable item of broken electronics by the neighbours once the word got round that there was a local lad that did repairs on the cheap. Knowing how to upsell would have been a useful skill then. Was this an entrepreneurial trait?

I continued with my education through various courses and whatever avenue of learning was available to me. With newly acquired skills I went on to develop several other ventures, and with each venture I learned something new that benefited me in the next one.

Although the drive to do something greater was always present, most of my ventures never grew beyond a hobby into a real business and, like a lot of people, I found that life's responsibilities take over and we put aside our dreams to pursue what is considered a meaningful career.

After many years in the corporate world I was introduced to the industry of Network Marketing, and the entrepreneurial cinders were ignited again. This time I was in an industry with other like-minded people, and I was exposed to what was to become the largest and most fundamental change in my life — the industry of personal development. This material has become an integral component of my life ever since and has provided me with the guidance and fortification that has carried me through business and personal setbacks.

Preface

My biggest success in business was followed by my biggest failure, with the collapse of the property market mid-2008. Trying desperately to hold onto a failing business, I watched several of my business colleagues collapse, and soon it was my turn. The failure cost me more than I had ever lost before, but hey, I was still in the game of life, preparing for the next opportunity. Isn't this what an entrepreneur does?

It was purely by chance that I developed an interest in online marketing when a friend invited me to take a look at his online business. I quickly realized that the game had changed massively from my first venture into MLM and direct marketing many years previously.

Technology had compressed the time frames. What would have once taken weeks, if not months, to develop could now be done in a matter of hours. But I soon found that many budding online entrepreneurs were desperately struggling. As with any business, whether it's bricks and mortar or online, one has to take the time to learn and understand the industry and be prepared to go through the learning curve. Fortunately, given the vast amount of information available on the Internet, one can gather this information quickly, and with careful research and due diligence can arrive at a conclusion in a short space of time.

My research led me to uncover the many Internet marketers who are led by what are called the Internet gurus. Romanticizing it with the lure of awaiting riches, they make it all look easy. But I can assure you it is not. You see, it's not about the gurus and how much money they are making; it's about you, and how much you are willing to develop personally.

There is a recipe for success and it starts by taking an inventory of where you are at this moment in time, knowing your starting point, your strengths and weaknesses. As good as any opportunity may be, one of the most valuable assets for success is a mentor. There is no point whatsoever starting an online business without a good mentor. This mentor could come in the form of engaging with a proven programme that provides coaching and a road map. If you speak to any successful person, they will tell you that they are continually investing in themselves, by seeking out others that are successful in their industry and learning from them.

But no matter how much desire you may have to start your online business, if you are not coachable then all the mentoring in the world is of no benefit.

In writing this book, I decided to call on my 35 years of experience in business and personal development and write a no-nonsense guide that

Preface

focuses on what I believe are the six fundamental traits for online success. My message to the many who enter this online industry every day, and the many still searching for success, is that one should not be looking for instant gratification because that is a shallow thought that has no substance. Rather one should approach the industry as you would any other business venture, and continually invest in yourself and your business and commit to staying the course.

I believe we are all born with an entrepreneurial spirit; I challenge you to look over your past and see if you recognize the entrepreneur spirit that is in you.

CHAPTER 1

DESIRE

If you are to become a successful Internet marketer, you are going to need one discipline in full measure before you even begin to learn the tricks of the trade for this job. You are going to have to make sure that you have a wellspring of this quality, that will sustain you through the inevitable ups and downs of Internet marketing and e-commerce. This discipline will have to drive you when you feel like giving up, when you want to sleep in and take a day off, when a deal goes bad and you feel cheated.

This "discipline" is actually a substance that is hard to define, but we all know what it looks like when we see it. This concept, almost a living entity, is desire.

The Role of Desire in Success

Desire will be what gets you started in e-commerce and it will be what sustains you in the early days when you are making less per hour than the barista at the coffee shop where you go to think of new ideas. Desire will be what you draw on again and again to continue to fulfil the vision you had when you quit your day job and thought it would be cool to make a living through a laptop. Well, you are going to have to see it as more than "cool". You are going to have to see it as a way to survive, a way to stay alive, and then, a way to prosper. Desire will motivate you, will push you and will guide you as you build your career as an Internet marketer. It is the absolutely essential ingredient that you will need to make a go of it in the crowded online world.

In fact, to be brutally honest, I must admit that the technological tricks that one marketer can play are not much different from the online know-how of the marketer right next door. What will often separate one budding entrepreneur from another one, in the online world or the real world, will be desire. Simply put, the e-commerce maverick with the greater desire will out-work and out-last the start-up founder who simply thought he had experienced enough desk work in a cubicle. In other words, the desire to leave the corporate world and work for yourself is not enough to sustain success. There has to be a deep-down burning yearning that will not be denied. That is called desire, and that is what will separate you from others who launch a website on the same day that you do.

Questions to Ask to Determine if You Have Sufficient Desire

To drill down a bit deeper into this question of desire, this mysterious need to succeed that you will have to have to survive the Internet jungle, it is helpful to look at what business experts say about the longing for achievement that you will need as you burst into the online world as a marketer.

In a recent article that has gained wide reading at Entrepreneur.com, Lisa Girard draws together the views of various experts to come up with "10 Questions to Ask Before Quitting Your Day Job to Run Your Own Company."[1] Many of the questions that she poses in this article touch on the desire that an Internet marketer will need in order to follow through on a strong beginning and to work hard for as long as it takes to make a good living on the Net. Desire will give you the initial courage to give your notice to your boss and launch out on your own. That's the first bold move that will separate you from the 70-80% of other workers that dream about leaving their job for something more fulfilling, as Jon Acuff notes in his book *Quitter: Closing the Gap Between Your Day Job & Your Dream Job.*[2]

The first relevant question that Girard suggests in her insightful article is: "Is this going to make me happier?"[3] This is a fantastic initial query, and Girard encourages anyone wanting to leave their day job to make sure that jumping into solo entrepreneurship is not just an escape from the drudgery of the daily routine under their office's fluorescent lights.

This dovetails beautifully with the need for desire — we will desire more fervently that which brings us pleasure and joy. You only have to think about your own life. The things that you desired the most were the ones that you thought would bring you the most pleasure and joy.

---

[1] Lisa Girard (2013), Entrepreneur, *http://www.entrepreneur.com/article/228183#ixzz 2f4CgYL8S*, retrieved 16.9.13.

[2] Jon Acuff (2011), cited in Girard, ibid

[3] Girard (2013)

Likewise, you need to have a good sense that Internet marketing will bring you pleasure and joy, or your desire will peter out. This means that your desire must go deeper than simply making money. You can make money in many ways if you work hard enough. If you don't like your day job you can go and sell cars or work on an oil rig or run your legs off waiting at tables in an expensive restaurant. If your only objective is to make money, there are a multitude of ways to do that outside of e-commerce. E-commerce must be a good fit for you if you are to pursue it to the fullest. If you are going to have the necessary reservoir of desire to propel you day after day into the Internet universe, you should draw some pleasure and joy from what the job of Internet marketer will call on you to do.

Use Passion to Fuel Your Desire

At the risk of using the far-overused "P" word, you will need passion to fuel your desire and keep on driving to success, whatever that looks like in your world. Obviously, this will vary according to the size of your vision. "Success" could mean simply covering your bills each month or it could mean making a six-figure income annually or even becoming an Internet millionaire. There is no guarantee that you will become a millionaire just by following the advice found in this book, however, if you do cultivate the six qualities explored here, you will certainly be successful on some level.

Back to passion. Many writers believe it is the essential force that you need to make any job work. I can use it as a synonym for desire in this chapter considering the observation of Chris Hurn, author of *The Entrepreneur's Secret to Creating Wealth: How the Smartest Business Owners Build Their Fortunes* who said "I personally believe you should get enjoyment out of your career [...] but before you go out to be your own boss, you have to believe you're going to be happier. If you can't say that you believe it will make you happier, don't do it."[4]

So, to recap thus far, the desire that will course through your brain and your veins must not be a negative desire, a desire to simply escape a difficult situation. It must be deeper and more positive than that, reaching down to another level of the soul. It must be a positive longing for something more in life: a rewarding career that brings joy and pleasure. The money will follow if this internal work is done in you.

---

[4] Chris Hurn (2012), cited in Girard (2013).

Desire

Get the Opinion of Family and Friends

Do you need some sort of external look at what is in your heart? No machine exists that will take a look into your soul, but friends and family around you can help you to determine if you might have what it takes to strike out on your own and begin an e-commerce business, or market for others with such businesses. Ask for the honest opinion of those around you to see if you have the traits described in this book — the six essentials to making it as an entrepreneur on the Net. As Acuff says in his book:

> Talking to family and close friends will help you realize if you're going after something that you really want to do, or just escaping your current situation. Don't just talk to the dreamers in the group that will tell you to go for it. Talk to the people that will be honest with you and encourage you if you're on the right path.[5]

That short quote contains a great amount of wisdom. You do not want to consult only with "yes men". You want to get the honest opinions of those who are closest to you and who will be the most radically impacted by your decision to fly solo. Their opinions will also be a handy double-check to verify that your "passion" is not simply a wish to escape from your current position.

This type of community involvement leads to another crucial point regarding the need for desire, which is that the desire should be shared by your significant others. If you are single and carefree, then you don't need to do this check, but if you are married or living with someone, if you have children or are responsible for providing for others' sustenance, then you should ensure that others are on board before you make your big move. If you are married, for instance, you need to have the backing of your wife or husband, otherwise you could be looking at business success and personal disaster. That story has been written many times before, but it does not need to be the case. A period of prolonged discussion that might involve some delicate negotiation is in order, to make sure that your mate is by your side and ready to do all s/he can to help you succeed. However, if you are coming out of a difficult financial situation, such as a medical emergency, the timing may not be right for joining the Internet entrepreneur crowd.

---

[5] Acuff (2011), cited in Girard (2013).

Desire

That's important for you to know, because even if you possess desire in spades, loved ones around you who do not share your vision could chip away at it little by little if they make discouraging remarks and complain about your minuscule profit in the early days of your business. If this harmful pattern continued, you might need to make a clear choice: your new career or your marriage/relationship. Giving you advice on that choice is outside the realm of this book, but you can help to avoid it by getting everyone around you on board before you give your notice and walk away from a regular job.

What Desire Produces

Having asked yourself a few hard questions and quizzed others around you to decide if you have a sufficient amount of desire to make it in the Internet world, you can move on to investigate what desire looks like in practical terms. Desire, in and of itself, is extremely difficult to capture in words. It is a burning feeling in your gut, a powerful emotion that gets you up at night and keeps you awake, a motivation that eliminates all distractions around you. It is not measurable, it is not quantifiable — you can't weigh it and you can't see it, touch it or feel it.

Image credit: <a href='http://www.123rf.com/photo_14575014_illustration-depicting-a-roadsign-with-an-ambition-concept-white-background.html'>72soul / 123RF Stock Photo</a>

Desire

What is a little easier to identify is the fruit of this kind of deep desire to succeed and to make it on your own. One of the most evident qualities that desire will produce in you is one that will be absolutely necessary in order to get an edge over the competition in Internet marketing: persistence. Nearly every successful Internet marketer who is asked about what it takes to achieve a comfortable living on the Web will tell you that persistence is vital.

The Vital Importance of Persistence

A recent article by Colleen DeBaise on "12 Personal Habits of Successful Marketers" gathering comments from successful entrepreneurs found that persistence was mentioned again and again. Eric Siu, CEO of Single Grain Digital Marketing, who has worked with the likes of Sony, Yahoo!, TurboTax and Random House, Inc., said of his key personal trait, "I am persistent. It's super-useful to be persistent with anything in life. You'll fail lots. You won't understand lots of things on the first try. But none of that matters because you know that if you persist, you'll get where you want to be initially."[6]

Siu's quote highlights clearly when you will need to draw on your desire to persevere through challenges. He acknowledges that failure WILL occur as you venture into Internet marketing, but that you should never let that deter you. Furthermore, he admits that even he has not understood many facts and truths about marketing, yet he did not let that stop him from growing a large company. His final sentence provides a rousing reminder of how desire can almost physically push us through to see the results we want: "…none of that matters because you know that if you persist, you'll get where you want to be initially." Nothing else matters, not failure, not lack of education or training, not rainy days or whiny clients. None of it matters as you persist, driven by your desire to stand on your own two feet and make a living as an Internet marketer.

A similar article summarizing the essentials for an Internet marketer has recently done the rounds, with the same qualities being emphasized there, too. This article made it onto birdherd.com — a site that gathers a lot of the best current information on Web marketing. The article, "The 10 Essential Qualities of a Successful Internet Marketer" is based on observations of

---

[6] Eric Siu, in article by Colleen DeBaise (2013) Entrepreneur, August 26, 2013. *http://www.entrepreneur.com/article/228059#ixzz2f490Q4dx*, retrieved 16.9.13.

marketers and discussions with them. It too praises the power of persistence, which I maintain grows out of a mile-deep foundation of desire:

> It is pure utopia to think that everything will run smoothly and perfectly the first time around. Successful people are persistent people. Success does not come from never falling, it comes from falling and getting back up successfully. Furthermore, great achievers have the ability to change failures into learning and creating opportunities.[7]

This idea, too, is worthy of analysis. You must anticipate failure and hardship as you begin to carve out a foothold in the crowded Internet marketing field. Yet, as you encounter difficulties of all sorts and fall occasionally, you should never stay down. The old saying about a winner being either a) up, or b) getting up, applies here. Desire that springs from a deep well will fuel your persistence above and through all obstacles.

Thus Internet marketing is not for the faint-hearted. It is not for the person who wilts under pressure, who crumbles under hardship, who quits when the going gets tough. Rather, it is for the person whose desire to succeed produces an unstoppable river of creativity, experimentation, good old-fashioned hard work, customer service and all sorts of other activities, who laughs in the face of danger and fights back.

Even with a burning desire to succeed, don't think for a moment that your desire cannot grow any more. Given enough hardship, you will either quit, or renew your aspiration to be a successful marketer. Desire produces persistence. If you are not a persistent person or doubt that you have sufficient desire to become one, then you most likely need to find another career to dabble in.

Desire Begets Determination

Another word that crops up repeatedly when successful marketers are asked what makes them tick is "determination". Think of determination as a sibling of persistence. They certainly come from the same family, borne of desire. Determination refuses to take "No" for an answer, it runs through barriers and is never deterred by them, it will not quit until the flag

---

[7] *http://birdherd.com/the-10-essential-qualities-of-a-successful-internet-marketer/*, retrieved 16.9.13.

is planted in the enemy territory. In your case, do not quit until *your* flag is planted, waving in the breeze and noted by everyone around you.

To quote from the revelatory article "Personality Traits Necessary for Success in Self-Employment", "Successful business owners view obstacles as challenges to overcome instead of walls that can't be climbed. To be successful, a self-employed person must be willing to face challenges when others take the 'easy road'."[8] In other words, determination sees "challenges" where others see "walls".

The last sentence of the quote highlights another quality that the person with a craving for success understands: they not only expect challenges, they face them down rather than quitting or trying to go around them.

In Internet marketing, this can be easy to do. Perhaps you have a troublesome client who refuses to act in good faith and you are wasting a lot of valuable time being stuck in a bad business deal. Rather than put off a confrontation with the client, you need to confront him/her and get the matter resolved. Even if you have to take a loss, you need to face up to this temporary obstacle and resolve the matter before it drains you of any more energy (and possibly sleep) or additional money.

Another example of facing down challenges rather than trying to get around them would be having one additional piece of technology that you need to master. Rather than putting off the mastery of that technology day after day, hoping that your need will dissolve with time, you need to wake up early and say "I will master this by the close of business today, whenever that will be," and set out to understand it inside and out. The desire to make it into the ranks of successful Internet marketers will produce that sort of single-minded determination, day after day after day, no matter what you need in order to thrive. You will not put off challenges for any length of time; you will confront them head-on, willing to take a few bruises in the process, but determined to wrestle the bear to the ground. That is determination.

Determination Makes the Difference

"Money-today.com" recently ran a great article on the "Six Important Qualities of a Successful Internet Marketer," and ranked determination to succeed as one of those top traits. Its analysis of this characteristic puts another spin on what has been discussed in the previous few pages:

---

[8] Patricia Gilliam (2007) Helium December 14, 2007. *http://www.helium.com/items/748091-personality-traits-necessary-for-success-in-self-employment*, retrieved 16.9.13.

Desire

> If you are determined to succeed, you WILL do what you need to do to succeed. People often start out strong but if it gets too rough, they quit. Please don't do this as there are always bumps in the road and you must push through them and always strive for success. We have seen so many times that people give up too early and if they would have kept going they would have seen amazing results and huge commission checks.

It makes the astute observation that the challenges Internet marketers face often come a while after that strong start. This can be especially devastating if you got off to a strong start and have become convinced that the rules don't apply to you — that your business growth will proceed smoothly upwards with no zags to accompany your zigs on the graph of income. Well, they will. The rules do apply to you. And, once you have been humbled and tumbled back to Earth, how will you respond? Will you quit, saying it is too hard? Or, will your desire multiply, providing sustenance to a determination that will not be denied.

There is a parable in the bible about good seed falling in the four different types of soil. Jesus noted that some plants spring up quickly but wither and fade when the sun beats down on them. He was using the parable to teach about different reactions to His Gospel message, but the same idea can be applied here. If your soil is of good quality and deep, then the plant, i.e. your business, will grow deep roots and not be susceptible to withering when the sun beams its merciless rays on your new creation. Desire is the deep, rich soil that keeps the business 'plants' going through drought and storms.

Another excellent article on the qualities needed to thrive as an Internet marketer was recently posted by Pakistani Internet marketer, Abdul Qadir Memon, showing the cross-cultural relevance of determination springing up out of desire:

> Rome wasn't built in a day! You have to keep trying and trying. Not all methods work or give results. You have to keep trying to get the results. If you aren't a determined person Internet Marketing is not for you. You must be able to keep up the hard work, and work until either you die or succeed. You must believe that one day your methods will work, and trust me, when Internet Marketing starts paying off it pays GOOD![9]

---

[9] Abdul Qadir Memon, Top 10 Qualities of an Internet Marketer, *http://qadirmemon.com/top-10-qualities-of-an-internet-marketer/*, retrieved 16.9.13.

"Success or death" might seem a little strong, but you get the point. No one is asking you to die for your career, but the determination that you will evince could indeed border on desperation. That's the sort of "want-to" that will wait for the large pay day while the groundwork is laid for sustained, generous earnings.

Desire Produces Focus

Persistence and determination are absolutely necessary for achievement in the sphere of Internet marketing, but if those qualities do not have a focus, you can end up as a scattered lone ranger, working on a variety of money-making schemes or sharing that passion with other domains of life, such as pastimes and favourite hobbies. Persistence and determination will not do you much good if you are distracted from the task at hand — building your business — and instead are pouring some of your best energy and time into improving your golf game or solving crossword puzzles, manicuring your lawn or trying to find the perfect pair of shoes.

Desire also produces a focus on a single objective, and it lets extraneous matters fall to the ground around it. It does not spend time trying to do many tasks well; rather, it has the fine tuning of a laser, pointed directly at the conquest of at least a share of the marketing world.

What does this focus look like in real life? One obvious sign of this focus will be the type of environment that you surround yourself with in your home office. It doesn't have to have every single piece of paper in place, but it does need to be a sacred spot, a place where work gets done and no distractions are allowed.

Entrepreneur.com's recent feature on "25 Common Characteristics of Successful Entrepreneurs" touched on this detail, which some might not consider important, but it absolutely is, and it reveals the focus you have, springing from your desire, to accomplish your goals as an Internet marketer.

Desire Affects Office Design

In terms of the design of your workspace, this article had an extremely practical summary:

> Carefully plan and design your home office workspace to ensure maximum personal performance and productivity and,

Desire

if necessary, to project professionalism for visiting clients. If at all possible, resist the temptation to turn a corner of the living room or your bedroom into your office. Ideally, you'll want a separate room with a door that closes to keep business activities in and family members out, at least during prime business and revenue generating hours of the day. A den, spare bedroom, basement or converted garage are all ideal candidates for your new home office. If this is not possible, you'll have to find a means of converting a room with a partition or simply find hours to do the bulk of your work when nobody else is home.[10]

You might not have thought that the design and layout of your home office could reveal anything about your level of desire to win, but it does. It can be helpful to look at your physical surroundings now and then to balance

Image credit: <a href='http://www.123rf.com/photo_14199728_senior-caucasian-man-working-from-home-in-shorts-with-desk-with-two-monitors.html'>backyardproduction / 123RF Stock Photo</a>

....

[10] James Stephenson, "25 Characteristics of Successful Entrepreneurs" *http://www.entrepreneur.com/article/200730#ixzz2f4BgpJBt*, retrieved 16.9.13

the philosophical statements on such intangible qualities as desire and focus outlined in this chapter. So, what are your plans for your office, or what does it look like now? Is it a corner of your bedroom? Do you really think that you can conquer the world from the corner of your bedroom?

Desire makes achievement a priority, and that means a corner of any room will not do. The advice about having a separate room is excellent, certainly one with a closing door. If you can't arrange that in your home or apartment, then rent a cheap office space where you can build your empire without constant interruption.

Desire Produces an Unquenchable Work Ethic

The aforementioned qualities in this chapter are all praiseworthy and important, but frankly, if they are not combined with a rugged work ethic, then you need to stay at your day job. You are going to need an iron-strong work ethic to make a stand in the world of Internet marketing. That ethic will spring out of your desire to be a hit and to make a living.

Most Internet marketers will tell you that the money did not flow immediately after their launch, no matter how heralded it was. They had to work like mad in the early days to build an empire. They had to neglect other duties for a time to get the ball rolling and help it to achieve enough momentum to knock over impediments down the line. Hopefully, you won't have to burn the midnight oil for years and years as an Internet marketer, but if you have a passion for it, you will actually enjoy your work and have to be called away from it by other crucial priorities, such as relationships and personal development.

As the earlier-cited article "10 Essential Qualities of a Successful Internet Marketer" states:

> A successful Internet Marketer is hard working and efficient: I am sorry to be the one bringing you the bad news but building a highly successful business that pays well requires hard work, at least in the beginning. Most very successful Internet Millionaires keep working although they do not need to just because they enjoy doing so.[11]

---

[11] birdherd.com, "10 Essential Qualities."

Desire

Many elements come together beautifully in this statement. The need for hard work is established, but the thought of hard work is tempered by the understanding that if Internet marketing is a good fit for you, if you can do it with passion and persevere, if you actually enjoy doing it, then "hard work" becomes a relative term. I will not go so far as to call it "play time", but it can be deemed as a pleasure overall if you are doing what you were made to do.

This brings us back to the first part of this chapter; if you have the desire to overcome anything in your path because you discover an enthusiasm for making a living in Internet marketing, then that desire can carry you a very long way. It can produce in you the persistence and determination needed to keep going even when the compensation is low. It will also produce a focus and seriousness about the entire transition into self-employment, ensuring that you give it your very best shot, pledging never to quit, no matter how discouraging the initial results.

Without desire, all of the "how-to"s in the world will not make you a rich Internet marketer. It is probably impossible to manufacture this desire; it needs to flow naturally as you consider the field of Internet marketing. Once it does, though, it can carry you to parts and heights unknown.

Do you have this innate desire? That's fundamental, but it's not all that you will need. Read on to discover the other five disciplines that you will need to call upon as you travel the road to happiness and wealth in Internet marketing.

CHAPTER 2

MOTIVATION

Now that I have fully examined the absolute necessity of desire as part of your make-up to become the next Internet marketing expert, I move on to a related quality that you also must have and maintain. Motivation is much like desire, but one difference is that your motivation can have multiple sources that can keep it high when you are tempted to flag a bit and perhaps even give up.

Desire is the starting point for a successful Internet marketing career; motivation flows out of that initial desire and is a kind of extension of it. Motivation is what gets you up in the morning and working throughout the day, rather than looking at Facebook for half the afternoon or taking a nap. Your motivation will need to stay at a consistently high level for you to make the splash that you desire on the Web and in the business world. So how do you keep it high? Fortunately, volumes have been written about how to maintain an elevated level of motivation, with a couple of sources that can vary according to who you are and where you are in your career.

How to Keep Your Self-Motivation Strong

I carried out an extensive survey of many of the top young entrepreneurs in Internet marketing and other fields in order to condense their advice and pass it on to you.

I begin with a look at a very helpful article on the popular website sixsigmaonline.org. The advice, entitled "Motivating Yourself as an Entrepreneur" has a wellspring of sound counsel for the budding boss of his/her own company.[1] It touches on the first source that is most mentioned in the analyses of what can keep an entrepreneur running on all cylinders — self-motivation. This is particularly important to tackle here first, because if you rely on outward motivators on a consistent basis, then starting your own business will probably not work, unless you are

---

[1] *http://www.sixsigmaonline.org/six-sigma-training-certification-information/motivating-yourself-as-an-entrepreneur.html*, retrieved 17.9.13.

Motivation

immediately stroked, rewarded and exalted in the early days of your business, a phenomenon that usually does not occur. The vast majority of successful entrepreneurs are amazingly self-motivated. They don't need anyone or anything outside of them to tell them to keep going; it comes from within, like an inexhaustible resource, an oil gusher that never stops.

As the author of that article states clearly in the opening section of this helpful piece:

> Entrepreneurs are generally driven people full of passion and seemingly limitless energy. But even the most driven gets to the point when all the passion just seems to fizzle out. There is a period when an entrepreneur might lose the interest and motivation to keep going; when all the external factors seem to be conspiring against the success of that entrepreneur. It is in such circumstances inner strength comes into play. Inner strength is the ability to keep going when it is easier and more convenient to give up. Inner strength means being able to self-motivate regardless of whether there is any external source of motivation or not.[2]

Several truths jump out of this quote, all of them worth noting:

1. You WILL run low on passion/desire at some point in the early stages of your business venture. You will run low on it during difficult days later in the game as well. Whenever you hit a plateau of some sort, in any activity that you are seeking to master, your desire can wane.

2. While you are running in quicksand on that plateau, you will need to draw deep on your self-motivation to soldier onward. The words "when all the external factors seem to be conspiring against success" should be memorized, because you will have those days, weeks and even months, perhaps seasons or years (hopefully not!). The word "conspiring" is especially meaningful, because it will feel that way at certain times, as if there is a conspiracy to curtail your success and drive for the top. Don't give in to that! It's false anyway. There is no conspiracy. People simply have bad days, as do computers, printers and all sorts of other things in the universe. Don't believe the phoney conspiracy theory, that your business "is just not meant to be". Lower your bucket into the well of self-motivation and brush off the bad days, the horrible weeks and the difficult months. Learn to laugh in the face of danger and keep going. Again, if you are the type of person

---
[2] Ibid.

who relies on outward strokes and lots of serendipity to keep going, then entrepreneurship of any kind is probably not for you.

3. The line about inner strength keeping us going "when it is easier and more convenient to give up" also leaps off the page. This means that growing your Internet marketing business will not be at all easy at times, and it will be much more convenient to just quit. Your inner motivation is going to have to carry you through such times, the times when a storm in your neighbourhood knocks out your power and the Internet for several days, the days when you are waiting to hear back from an investor, the days when several prospective clients decline your services. Those days come, and then they go. Your inner self-motivation will be key to keeping on, and not quitting.

Advice from Top Entrepreneurs on Keeping Motivation High

The article goes on to give sage advice on how to keep your self-motivation up and your enthusiasm bubbling:

1. Stay focused on the finish line, not only where you foresee your business in 10 years, but working backward from an answer to a problem through the difficulties. This is a helpful sales technique as well: getting a client to look at where s/he wants to go, then working through how to get there while anticipating problems.

2. As part of that focus on the end result, you must allow yourself to feel satisfied with the effort that you give each day. As Ciara Vesey, creator of "Confessions of a Law School Nobody" said about what keeps her motivated: "Reaffirming to myself what the 'endgame' is keeps me motivated. I also made an agreement to always do my best each and every day such that no particular day can be called a failure."[3]

3. Formulate clear and well-defined goals. I will examine this in greater detail in the next chapter of this book on 'planning'. The old saying about aiming at nothing and hitting it comes to mind. If you have clear, measurable goals, you will be able to discern if you are making progress towards those goals. Even on terrible days, you will still be able to see that you are marching towards your goal, as a few good days make up for one or two horrific ones. Congratulate yourself when you make progress, ANY

[3] Ibid.

Motivation

progress, and feed your inner drive with a bit of encouragement. Keep a record of the encouragement that others give you as well!

4. Part of keeping a record of that encouragement might be enhancing the feedback channels to your site and business. Open up the pipeline. Yes, it is a risk. You might hear a lot of chatter that you don't want to hear but you might also receive suggestions that could make your enterprise stronger. What you will also receive is unexpected encouragement from happy clients and customers. As Vincent Ko, the co-founder of Panda sunglasses advises:

> Establish strong, yet effortless communication channels for your customers to provide you feedback (an easy-to-find email, occasional surveys, sending a personal email to a customer, social media, etc). Not only is this a good customer service practice, but you will be surprised by the number of purchasers who are advocates of your brand. Receiving positive feedback and reassuring messages from happy customers is inspirational and keeps me motivated.[4]

5. The co-founder and CEO of giant Her Campus Media, Stephanie Kaplan, looks to a different place for her motivation. She advocates a system where you set increasingly higher goals to add logs to the fire of your motivation. As she recently stated, "Keep setting higher and higher goals for yourself. Any time you reach a goal you have set, rather than pat yourself on the back and become complacent, immediately set a next, even more ambitious goal for yourself, so you always have something you are working towards."[5]

6. Maise Knowles, the co-founder and COO of FreeShipping.org, shares a similar philosophy about goal-setting and motivation: "Set goals – at the beginning of every year establish at least one goal you'd like to work towards. Try to stretch yourself professionally to meet that goal, and ensure you don't make it unrealistic or too easily achievable."[6]

7. This leads to another key point: surround yourself with positive people. You don't need clients who may act as constant sprinklers on the fire that

---

[4] Ibid.

[5] Ibid.

[6] Ibid.

Motivation

Image credit: <a href='http://www.123rf.com/photo_2616013_ethnically-diverse-businesspeople-sitting-at-table-in-restaurant-talking.html'>iofoto / 123RF Stock Photo</a>

burns within you. You don't need partners that have an "Eeyore" outlook (think "Winnie the Pooh"). You also don't need a crowd of "yes" men or women. You should find people who inspire you, not demoralize you. You know the difference! Joe Martin of Merchandize Liquidators, LLC says that he stays motivated by "Socializing with successful people. By socializing with people that are more successful than you are, it will give you a mental push and help break that mental barrier that's stopping you from actually making millions."[7]

8. No one, of course, can promise that you will make "millions" if you simply hang around the right people, but entrepreneurs of all kinds constantly talk about socializing and circulating with like-minded people who are on a similar path in life, people who are not waiting for action to happen, but who make the action themselves. Juanita Hines, owner of Regional Consulting, puts it this way: "Surround yourself with people who are

---

[7] Ibid.

Motivation

striving and pursing success for themselves and those who will encourage you to succeed in life as well."[8]

9. This doesn't mean that you have to spend every waking hour with high-energy people. You might like to have friends who know nothing about your world as an Internet marketer. However, it can do wonders for your motivation and creativity to spend at least some time with members of your "tribe", the entrepreneurial pack of people in your city or region who are too self-motivated to work in a cubicle. Andrew Woo, the founder and CEO of ProspectSnap, highly recommends at least an occasional happy hour or dinner with tribal brothers and sisters:

> You can get a huge boost of energy by going out to happy hour or dinner with other entrepreneurs or startups. A great new site for this is GrubWithUs. I met some really awesome people that gave me tons of ideas for marketing my app, and some key introductions to others that could help me too.[9]

Adam Martin, founder of Laabn Social Haircare Inc., takes it a step further, arguing for a relationship of accountability with someone who has embarked on the same journey that you have, inside or outside the Web. "This is a crucial step I take. Look for another business owner in the same or totally different profession that you can talk to on a weekly or daily basis if possible, to discuss ideas, challenges, and triumphs," he says. "This is a great way to keep both parties accountable".

There is much truth in this concept. When you are tempted to pack it in, or simply sleep away three days at a time, having an accountability partner can help you to stay on track and remain encouraged. When someone else is tempted to quit, we often react by seeking to talk him/her out of it. Likewise, when you are tempted to go back to pushing paper and being bored for eight hours a day, you will need a buddy to snap you out of it.

Even though Internet commerce can be seen as quite a solo flight, it actually can and should involve other people in your journey. You should not only write in social hours with other like-minded people on a regular basis, you might want to set up a weekly check-in time with someone who is also building a business. Don't go easy on your new friend, and don't let

---

[8] Ibid.

[9] Ibid.

him/her go easy on you! Ask the hard questions. Make each other better. Spur each other on and see what happens.

Don't Ever Forget that Day You Quit

10. Remember the day you decided to launch out on your own. Recall why you made the crazy move to quit your day job in the first place. Remember how much you dreaded working in that cubicle. Remember how often you got so angry with your supervisor you could not get to sleep at night. Remember what others told you about having an entrepreneurial spirit. Remember your mate telling you that you just don't work well for others, that you are probably way too smart to be an underling. Remember all of this when you are ready to give up.

Betsy Hauser, founder and president of Flexiruggz LLC, affirms the strength of this source of motivation. She says that she remains committed to her entrepreneurial journey through "Visiting my friends at their offices and seeing them working in cubicles. That sort of corporate lifestyle is the exact thing I don't want with my life because it would stifle my creativity and keep me from expanding my horizons and success!"[10]

According to Ross Johnson, CEO of 3.7 Designs:

> Nothing is more motivating than considering the alternative of being self-employed. Building value for someone else's company, being controlled by a boss, only being able to influence your success rather than being in full control of it. Picturing this scenario is enough to turn the worst day into an empowering one.[11]

Another twist on this source of motivation might be to remember the reaction of your superiors when you announced that you were leaving the comforts of corporate life to strike out on your own. You might have really liked your colleagues at your former job, and they might have wished you well on your future success. You might even continue to socialize with them.

---

[10] http://www.sixsigmaonline.org/six-sigma-training-certification-information/motivating-yourself-as-an-entrepreneur.html.

[11] Ibid.

Motivation

Ah, but the boss. Do you remember his or her reaction? That combined look of puzzlement, pity and you-will-regret-this attitude. That might be the person you need to think most about when you are tempted to give up. Do you really want to go back to "Robocorp" and beg for your old job back, just because you've hit a few snags in your master plan?

Image credit: <a href='http://www.123rf.com/photo_18025241_closeup-portrait-of-a-young-business-man-with-head-tilted-to-a-side-is-looking-at-the-camera-suspici.html'>feedough / 123RF Stock Photo</a>

As Jill Nadorlik, the president of Nadorlik & Co., points out: "Thinking back to the look on my former bosses' faces when I told them I wanted to start my own company. I envision them slaving away at the job they hate, chained to their desks. It puts a smile on my face to know that I'll never have to report to them again."[12]

If that face doesn't motivate you, nothing will!

---

[12] Ibid.

Motivation

Even if you don't remember what your boss looked like when you walked out on the final day, you can remember your critiques of that boss and how you resented him or her having complete control over your ascendancy on the corporate ladder. One of the great benefits of being an Internet marketer is that you will determine in large part how rapidly you rise up the ladder of earnings.

As Dana Kaye, owner of Kaye Publicity, puts it:

> I am motivated by the fact that I have total control over my career. I'm not at the mercy of an employer or owner with poor judgment who makes flawed decisions. It's up to me how many clients I take on, the hours I work, and the company's culture and style. If I'm ever upset or frustrated about my job, I always remind myself of this control and it motivates me to keep growing my business.[13]

Bisera Urdarevik, founder of Lush Gourmet Foods, LLC, adds another dimension to this "show 'em" attitude. "Starting a small business at a young age presents many obstacles and skeptics just looking to see how successful you can really be," he notes. "That said, it's my biggest motivational tool — wanting to prove those people wrong. Why not be able to establish a business at 21 and be more successful than others doing the same in their 30s, 40s, and up?"[14]

This desire to show that youth is *not* always wasted on the young might be a powerful motivator for you. It's no accident that many Internet entrepreneurs get their start in their early 20s. At the same time, you should never discount your chance at success simply based on your age. Plenty of other people are checking out of cubicle life and checking into solo entrepreneurship in their 30s, 40s, 50s and beyond.

Self-Motivation and the Internet Marketer

This outstanding advice for refreshing your motivation applies to all sorts of entrepreneurs, but much has been written about the particular challenges for Internet entrepreneurs as well. Online-money-today.com gave this pep talk in an article on the "Six Important Qualities of a Successful Internet Marketer":

---

[13] Ibid.

[14] Ibid.

Motivation

Being self-motivated is the only way that you will succeed. The motivation must come from within. If you are only externally motivated then you will only make it so far. If you are internally motivated, then you have a fire inside you that will not burn out and you will see results in your business and make huge Internet commissions.[15]

The key point to take from this is the notion that you can indeed make it to a certain point as an Internet marketer by relying primarily on external motivation. Perhaps you will have an early payday, be able to raise big money through Kickstarter.com, or any other number of scenarios that can get you off to a blazing start. Yet, as the rush of the launch wears off, you will eventually need the "fire inside you that will not burn out" to continue to pursue your goals. If you get into Internet marketing and realize that you are not internally motivated, you can always quit, hopefully without having thrown away all of your savings or investment money. No one who has succeeded in Internet marketing would deny that self-motivation is a central factor crucial for success.

Think Big magazine provides this funny and ultra-practical advice regarding self-motivation:

> When you're an employee, other people tell you what to do, either directly or indirectly. You get used to having your actions directed by others. But you have to direct your own actions as a small business owner. You can't just sit there and hope that maybe some clients stroll in or that someone will drop by out of the blue with inventory for your retail store. No one's going to drop work on your desk or point out what needs to be done. For many people who try to become self-employed and start businesses after having a long-term full-time job, this is the hardest adjustment to make. Being able to do whatever it takes to get the jobs done is essential. And marketing has to be your best friend. People just don't walk in the door, yet lots of small business owners think they do, and when it's not busy they're happily reading a magazine or on Facebook wasting the day.[16]

---

[15] *http://online-money-today.com/6-important-qualities-of-a-successful-internet-marketer/*, retrieved 16.9.13.

[16] From *http://www.thinkbigmagazine.com/business/254-successfully-self-employed*, retrieved 16.9.13

Motivation

Although this is referring to a bricks-and-mortar operation, it holds true for the Internet entrepreneur as well. It can be quite an adjustment from having your agenda set for you by an employer each day to setting your own agenda each day. Some of you will be coming out of employment situations where nearly every minute was externally directed; others of you maybe had some freedom to set your own schedule as long as the work got done. In either case, being your own boss and deciding how you will use each minute can be either thrilling or extremely challenging.

The truth that "No one's going to drop work on your desk" is another true maxim. They will not! You will have to go out and get it, and you will need to be internally motivated to do that on a regular basis.

As for marketing being your best friend, you understand that already if you hope to become a wealthy Internet marketer! Don't neglect your own marketing as you help others meet their goals through your expert advice.

The final line on magazines and Facebook is also important. It might be a good idea to keep the magazines away from your work space and designate a set time that you will go on Facebook each day. Otherwise, you can waste hours keeping up with friends —and not making any money doing it.

Perhaps one of the biggest names in Internet marketing would have some wisdom to share about the necessity of self-motivation. Neil Patel, co-founder of Crazy Egg and KISSmetrics, says:

> Running a business is like riding on a roller coaster. Although it is fun and exciting, there will be times when you'll be scared and feel powerless. During the bad times there isn't much you can do, other than to keep on *pushing forward*.[17]

One can see how Patel has got to where he is today. It is about just pushing forward through the bad times! The image of a roller coaster might come in handy as you go through the inevitable ups and downs of launching and running your own business. If Patel has felt powerless at times, you will too. If he has experienced bad times, then you can expect them as well.

---

[17] *http://yfsentrepreneur.com/2012/07/19/35-entrepreneurs-share-how-they-stay-motivated-in-business/#ixzz2f9ZKiiiR*, retrieved 17.9.13

Motivation

Patel's insight brings to mind a strong quote from former Prime Minister Winston Churchill: "Success is not final, failure is not fatal: it is the courage to continue that counts."[18]

You will need that courage to keep getting up when you are knocked down or even thrown out of the roller coaster. That courage comes from a fervent self-motivation that can't be doused by any external factor. Please do not consider these quotes as some sort of college pep talk to get you whipped into a lather and quit your 9-to-5. They are, instead, nuggets of truth whose veracity will be borne out in time as you embark on Internet entrepreneurship.

Likewise, it can be helpful to find out from peers what keeps them self-motivated. To save you the time needed for texting, emailing or even calling some of the brightest minds in the field, I have compiled several quotes from them regarding the vital nature of self-motivation. Given that we are all different and that different ideas will resonate with some of us more than others, hopefully you will find something of value on these next few pages. It's always good to hear from people who have succeeded rather than those who have flailed and failed, as some of your local friends or old college roommates possibly have.

There's Always Tomorrow

Here is what several successful entrepreneurs had to say about keeping the self-motivation flame burning brightly:

Erika A. Salter, the founder/executive producer of Salter Entertainment Group LLC, focuses on the one-day-at-a-time theme:

> "Each new day brings an opportunity to get it right." This mantra simply means if you don't accomplish all your goals, to-do lists, or even land that big sales contract, there is always tomorrow to get it right. Tomorrow always brings a new opportunity to be better, stronger, more efficient, and get it right. Simple and true.[19]

The promise of tomorrow can indeed be an important part of self-motivation. As long as you see your "failures" as teaching opportunities,

---

[18] Ibid.

[19] Ibid.

Motivation

you can get up, brush yourself off and determine to get it right the next day. Again, notice that successful people often mention failure as they talk about success. It is unavoidable unless you are King Midas, but it does not have to mean the termination of your aspirations.

An important part of self-motivation must begin with at least a measure of self-confidence. You must believe in yourself to some degree if you are going to succeed as an Internet marketer. As you draw down into your soul for self-motivation, there must be some reservoir of confidence that will convince you to keep on trying even after failures, large or small.

Positive Attitude Plays a Role

Alberto Armijo, co-founder of VocaBoca and Noneed2call, shares a couple of positive-attitude statements that keep him pressing on amidst difficulty: "'Today will be the day' and 'If this idea does not work I have 4 or 5 more to try.' I get up visualizing that my apps will get really popular soon and, if they do not work as expected, I will just develop another idea that will be successful."[20]

That last statement merits particular attention. It begins with a very sunny outlook on any given business day — "I get up visualizing that my apps will get really popular soon" — and ends with a resolute attitude that refuses to be discouraged: "I will just develop another idea that will be successful." What an incredible mindset.

Apply it to your work as an e-commerce newbie. You need to wake up believing that you will learn a little each day about mastering the money-making end of e-commerce, that you will take advantage of a new tip, that you will begin to use a new type of advertising, whatever the case may be.

As you look at data at the end of the day and notice that you did not get the number of page views that you had hoped for, or you receive an email from a prospective advertiser declining your offer, you can have one of two reactions. You can either conclude, "I'm not meant for this. I need to quit", or you can respond positively: "Tomorrow I will do this better and get more page views sometime in the near future" or "I need to work on my advertising pitch, or even find businesses that fit into my niche better so that sales will be much easier".

---

[20] Ibid.

Motivation

Your positive attitude will keep the well of self-motivation fairly full. A negative attitude will drain it. You will have many opportunities to believe that you will fail and that you are, yourself, a failure. Don't give in to these thoughts!

I'm not referring to some sort of strange mind game or pop psychology. What I am trying to communicate is that every Internet marketer faces bumps in the road; every entrepreneur has times of failure. It's how you respond to these inevitable times of letdown that will ultimately play a key role in your success or lack thereof. Take a cue from Armijo: have the confidence that tomorrow you will find the right key to unlock achievement in your given area of the commercial world. If you believe that accomplishment will inevitably follow hard work and learning as you go, fuelled by the desire described in chapter 1, then you will be far more likely to actually triumph in your quest to establish a solid foothold in e-commerce.

Consider the Competition

Another way to think about this is that at the same time as you are considering quitting and/or your start-up money is about to run out, someone else is indeed signing off and going back to the corporate world. Another newbie is deciding to push harder. That person is your competition.

Need a new jolt of self-motivation? John Ostman, the vice-president of sales/marketing and creative director of Probus OneTouch/Snap Agency, keeps in mind the competition when his self-motivation could ebb. This, by the way, is a common motivator for many world-class athletes. They want to be on the field, in the gym, working out, running, lifting, etc., at all the hours that their future opponents are not. If that means getting up at 5 a.m. for a run, they do it. If that means practising penalty kicks on a darkened field near midnight, then they do that.

Ostman puts it this way:

> If I don't take the initiative to act, someone else will. I keep a notepad next to my bed so that I can capture those late night or middle-of-the-night ideas and act on them the next day. Motivation is telling myself that "there may be better ideas out there, but I will not be out-worked by my competitors".[21]

---

[21] Ibid.

Motivation

If you are the type of person that thrives on competition, rather than shrinking from it, this insight should get your blood flowing! To think that others might be writing down the Next Big Idea in the middle of the night while you simply toss and turn or get up to take a sleeping pill is sobering. Self-motivation wants to out-work the competition. And, I soberly remind you, there is plenty of competition out there.

Millions of people, young and old, believe that they have what it takes to be a self-made millionaire. Most of those people are running to the Web to make those dreams come true, and hundreds of thousands of them have heard that there is easy money to be made in Internet marketing. That means that the Internet is literally crawling with people trying to make a fortune, many of them in marketing. Yes, there is plenty of competition out there for you. The question is, do you have the self-motivation to beat those who are competing for the same clients as you are? Ostman's notion can help you find what you need deep in your soul in order to come out on top.

Putting Your Own Cash on the Line

Of course, other ways to stay self-motivated could involve perhaps one of the biggest motivators of all: not friends, not self-belief, not the competition even, but putting your own savings on the line. If at all possible, use fantastic crowd-funding websites such as kickstarter.com and others to grab the capital you need to launch, but if you really want to safeguard your sky-high, initial motivation, put your own money into the pot as well.

It can be far easier to be lazy when we are "playing" with someone else's money. We get a lot more serious when we are trying to make our own money grow. If you don't believe me, go to a casino and use a friend's money and see what you do. You'll traipse from one table to the next, trying your hand at roulette, black jack, poker and other amusements. You'll have a wonderful time with nothing to lose, and if all of the money goes up in a puff of smoke, you will feel a little guilt, but probably simply chalk it up to experience and savour the exciting night in the casino.

When it's $1,000 of your own money? You will play only the games that you know how to play, and that will occur after you have spent months studying how to win at black jack. Your attitude will be entirely different when your own resources are on the line. No more casual strolling around with a huge grin on your face. That will be replaced by a steely determination to win.

Motivation

Likewise, if you are going to be an Internet marketer, you might need to include some or all of your savings to make it more real to you and to get your body out of bed when you are tempted to sleep in another day because you have the sniffles. As Nolan Watson, president and CEO of Sandstorm Gold Ltd. puts it: "Put your personal money on the line" to supply the self-motivation that you need.[22]

Lindsay Saewitz, founder of CitySwarm, says: "Being self-funded, money is a big motivator ... If I don't work, I can't do all the fun things I want to do."[23]

Fun and doing what you want to do to find it needs to be kept in mind when you are putting your nose to the proverbial grindstone when no one is watching. If you are self-funded, as many entrepreneurs are, you will be much more likely to hang on when the going gets tough.

Looking Back, Straight Ahead and Forward for Motivation

Other entrepreneurs remark on the different ways that they re-stoke their motivation by making reference to the past, the present and the future. If you still haven't found the right source for continuing your motivation, consider the perspectives offered below. Some of us are more forward-looking thinkers, focusing on the future. Some of us make a point of living in the moment. Others look to the past for motivation. Wherever you look — past, present or future — you can often find new wellsprings of motivation if you try.

Mike Calloway, founder of Trinity Digital Marketing, says that a few thoughts about all of the hard work that he has put into his business in the past help him to keep going. You might try this perspective when you are tempted to quit, recalling the crazy hours and your own money that you have sunk into your new career before deciding to pack it in. As Calloway puts it: "Knowing that nothing great or worth having has ever happened easily, fast, and without hard work. For sustained success, you must put in continuous hard work. If I ever decided to quit, it could be just one opportunity away from breakthrough and all the labor done up until then would have been wasted."[24]

---

[22] Ibid.

[23] Ibid.

[24] Ibid.

Motivation

Other entrepreneurs focus on the given day and break down the enormity of growing a business into bite-sized pieces. This approach encourages a focus on the day, to seize it, along with every moment within that day. This could be a valuable source of continual motivation for you.

Will Curran, president of Endless Entertainment, says he gets motivation "by fighting the small battles. I get joy in overcoming obstacles, and by celebrating after a small win. This includes rewarding myself for a job well done. You can get overwhelmed by focusing too much on the big picture."[25]

This sounds like a nice balance to the mindsets discussed earlier in this chapter, where reference to the bigger picture tended to be the focus. Don't forget to celebrate the many small victories. Often we can get overwhelmed by the small failures; they can even ruin our day and our psychological health if we let them. Let the smaller wins resonate in your heart and soul, at least for a few moments. What kind of reward can you give yourself for signing up that new client or mastering that new technology? How about a trip to a coffee shop or a movie rental? Whatever is your particular thing, be sure to focus not only on the difficult moments but on the moments of joy as well.

J.P. Bauman, executive vice president of AudioGlove, echoes this sentiment:

> Instead of only acknowledging achievement of the final goal, breaking down projects into smaller milestones and finding ways to celebrate their completion along the way is important for building morale and motivation. It gives me and my team a sense of accomplishment and keeps us charging hard towards the ultimate goal.[26]

Part of this system of personal rewards could be to do something you really enjoy each day as a way of reminding yourself that, as a self-employed person, you can actually take a bit of time out of your day to do something that makes you happy. The guy stuck in the cubicle each day can't go out for a long walk whenever he feels like it; the woman who lives on deadline pressure every week has a very hard time taking half an hour off to read a magazine article in bed. These are the types of small treats you might need to keep your motivation at a healthy level.

---

[25] Ibid.

[26] Ibid.

Motivation

Brandon Wu, founder of Studio Pepwuper, puts it this way:

> Do one thing every day that excites you – we are often so bombarded with routines and tasks that we forget what excited us in the first place to start our businesses. Finding things that excite you and doing them every day reminds you why you started the business and helps keep the motivation up.

Beyond this day-to-day system of personal rewards and celebration of small wins comes a look to the future. If the current state of your Internet business is sorry, as Annie says, "There's always tomorrow".

Josh Neblett, CEO of GreenCupboards, has this take on finding motivation in the future, "Find new opportunities. As an entrepreneur the moment you become complacent and accept where your business currently stands is the day it's time to move on. Motivation and drive comes from within but you add fuel to the fire by constantly seeking perfection."[27]

Justin Palmer, founder and CEO of MedSaverCard, takes a really long-term view to find the motivation to stay disciplined day in and day out as he builds his business:

> Thinking about the future freedom and time it will allow me to spend with my family. Entrepreneurship is hard work and requires sacrifice, sometimes putting off things you'd rather be doing in the moment. But if you build your business right now, it will provide freedom and wealth for years to come. Traditional employment, while it may be easier and safer in the moment, will never provide this kind of future value for you.[28]

There's a lot to chew on in that little nugget! When you are getting stressed and tired by the amount of time that you are pouring into your fledgling business, perhaps you need to look far, far down the road and envision a future where you have all kinds of time off and can make friends and family the priority they should be. The idea that Palmer wants to communicate is that this risk that you have chosen to take has a pay-off far greater than that which is offered to those who simply play it safe in a stable job.

---

[27] Ibid.

[28] Ibid.

Motivation

Finding Motivation Through Customer Satisfaction

Another school of thought within this quest to find the needed motivation for keeping at it and building a business can be the sheer pleasure that you can draw out of meeting the needs of your clients and customers. Many Internet entrepreneurs find a deeper motivation here, a motivation more profound than can be conjured through thoughts of personal happiness or wealth. You might be one of those people who simply enjoy making others happy. If so, you will be joining many other Internet marketers who get a thrill out of meeting a need and helping others in the process.

A lot of Internet experts claim that they do it all for their customers. Who are we to doubt? Jason Falls of CafePress says:

> I have a genuine interest in people and what triggers them to want to both buy and advocate for a brand. To me, marketing is not about selling. It's about cultivating an audience of passionate friends who both do business with and for you. It's a utopian notion, but not impossible to achieve.[29]

Is this a "utopian notion"? It might sound nearly impossible to you as you chase down payment from one client and get into a nasty email scrap with another. Karen Leland of Sterling Marketing Group would say that part of your problem with troublesome clients is failure to realize that not every client is the right client. As she puts it:

> I have absolute certainty that not every potential client is the right fit. This keeps me from spending time trying to convince someone to work with me. Instead I look for a natural fit and obvious connection. This makes for the happiest and most successful client relationships in the long run.[30]

This is great advice and should not be taken lightly. Even in your desperation to build your Internet marketing business, you might realize, upon further reflection, that certain clients are taking a lot of the joy out of your workday. You might need to establish a set of criteria for any new client, or you might need to be far more sensitive to your hunches when you are considering an engagement with a new client. You can often get a sense of how well the relationship is going to go through early emails,

---

[29] *http://www.entrepreneur.com/article/228059#ixzz2f4AKiNif*, retrieved 23.9.13.

[30] Ibid.

Motivation

Skype interviews and other forms of communication. Don't discount those feelings of dread that you have as you go back and forth with a prospective client on what you think is a simple matter! That might be your heart's way of telling you, "Don't go there!" You will be far happier in the long run if you choose to bypass such clients rather than see them as future income.

Once you find a stable of clients with whom you mesh well, perhaps you will be half as inspired as Peter Shankman of the marketing firm ShankmanHonig:

> I have a deep-seeded desire to make people smile. Seriously. It's the same desire that got me branded as "Class Clown" in school and got me in trouble. But as an adult, it helps. I can figure out what a person needs, and figure out a way to get it. I'm not afraid to take the gamble – get up at 4 a.m. to get online to bring a "cronut" to a meeting, for example, or take a client skydiving. Once you've gotten a client's trust and made them smile, doing business with them is the easy part.[31]

You don't necessarily have to be a skydiver to experience the joy of helping others reach their goals as you reach yours. You don't even have to know what a "cronut" is. Just go back to one of the first maxims of business: "It's all about the customer."

As *Entrepreneur* magazine reminded home-based business owners in a recent article:

> Your home business is not about the products or services that you sell. Your home business is not about the prices that you charge for your goods and services. Your home business is not about your competition and how to beat them. Your business is all about your customers, or clients, period. After all, your customers are the people that will ultimately decide if your business goes boom or bust. Everything you do in business must be customer focused, including your policies, warranties, payment options, operating hours, presentations, advertising and promotional campaigns and website. In addition, you must know who your customers are inside out and upside down.[32]

---

[31] Ibid.

[32] *http://www.entrepreneur.com/article/200730#ixzz2f4B2p2WD*, retrieved 23.9.13.

Motivation

That's a great reminder when thinking about sources of motivation to keep the flame lit in your heart and mind. Megan Allen, co-founder of Georgie Beauty, has similar advice:

> Connect with your customers. They are the reason you started your business, and they are the reason you're successful. When I'm feeling burned out, I spend an afternoon in a Neiman Marcus or Nordstrom that sells our beauty products, and I talk to customers directly. By simply connecting with our customers, I feel inspired and motivated. In a world that is dominated by smart phones and social networking, a little face time goes a long way.[33]

It might not be possible to ever make such face-to-face contact with your clients a reality. You might have the majority of your clients on another continent, or they could be in a distant city far from your location. However, if you are able to break through the layers that separate you from your customers, it can be a true thrill to meet them and hear how your business is making a difference in their lives. That might be just the reminder you need to stay on course and continue to build your business.

In fact, some experts would say that customer satisfaction needs to be at the very foundation of your motivation if you are to succeed in the long run. There might be some truth to that, as many psychologists would say that in pleasing and serving others we find the deepest satisfaction, that living for self is not the ultimate source of deep contentment. I wholeheartedly believe this is why we should strive to develop our charitable values.

A group of Internet marketers who were polled for a recent article about qualities of successful marketers produced this counsel:

> "A successful Internet Marketer honestly cares about his customers":
>
> > This one may come as a shocker. It is true though that successful marketers are in business because they care about making a difference and helping their customers. A person may make a good sum of money while selling a low-quality service or product once. On the long run though, the customers can see through this person's facade and recurring income is not going to be at the "rendez-vous".

---

[33] http://www.entrepreneur.com/article/228059#ixzz2f4AKiNif

Motivation

> Action: Examine your profound motives in wanting to do Internet Marketing. Are you just 'trying' this to get out of a job you do not like? Is helping other people through the products and services you are providing a genuine goal for you?[34]

That's a pretty tough reality check, but I recommend it. Again, as has been noted in both these first two chapters, escaping an undesirable job is not the best source of motivation to get into Internet marketing. You should have the desire to service clients and possess an entrepreneurial streak that can withstand the many ups and downs in this business.

Helim.com, a popular business site, included such desire for customer satisfaction in its formula for business success, in a recent post entitled "Personality Traits Necessary for Success in Self-Employment". If you are struggling mightily with flagging motivation, perhaps you need to go back to square one and decide if you have the traits described below:

> Business owners tend to be more extroverted and friendly toward people. That doesn't mean a shy or introverted person can't be successful in self-employment, but they may have to develop skills with people according to their field of business. This can also happen over time with practice.
>
> Self-employed people are likely to be empathetic toward others. Recognizing needs that people have can be the first step in developing a successful business. Even in the rare instance of dealing with an upset customer, you often have to put yourself in their position to solve the problem and ease tension.[35]

If All Else Fails

Finally, if all else fails to give you the pick-me-up that you need to keep on pressing toward the goal, consider keeping a file of quotes that get your motor running again. You can draw such quotes from this book, from sources you find on the Net, or from other books that you have read about entrepreneurship and/or Internet marketing. You can even write down or

---

[34] http://birdherd.com/the-10-essential-qualities-of-a-successful-internet-marketer/

[35] http://www.helium.com/items/748091-personality-traits-necessary-for-success-in-self-employment, retrieved 25.9.13.

Motivation

cut and paste encouragement that you have received from clients or others related to your business. You can also follow me on twitter Pat_headley, and get my daily motivational tweets.

All of these notes of encouragement can help you to persevere when you are tempted to fold. As Nick Herinckx, CEO of Obility Consulting, advises:

> Keep a small text file on your computer desktop where you keep a list of inspiring quotes you run across, and then read this list once per week to really stay energized. Even during tough times, by reading the list of quotes I have collected, I'm reminded why I started my own business and that I'm not alone in business or challenges I face.[36]

No, you are not alone. Thousands and thousands of other people a lot like you have taken the risk and dived into Internet marketing. Whether you find renewed motivation through gatherings with other marketers, inspirational quotes, a mental image of your boss's face when you quit, or the joy in helping a customer to get what s/he needs, turn to the sources that replenish your fire the most. I hope that this chapter has helped you to decide to keep on building your career, or, if necessary, has perhaps shown you that a move into Internet marketing is not for you.

---

[36] *http://www.entrepreneur.com/article/228059#ixzz2f4AKiNif*

CHAPTER 3

PLANNING/GOAL-SETTING

When I decided to embark on an Internet marketing career, I didn't leave anything to chance. Every aspect of my business was charted to make sure I had clear goals, that I stayed the course during times of trouble and would know how to overcome any obstacles I might face.

As a self-employed individual, there will be challenges ahead – and you will be the only one responsible for dealing with them. Unlike in the business world, there will be no supervisor to blame.

When the going gets tough, you'll be able to confront difficulties head-on with the guidance of a solid business plan. Your business plan will also help you know if you're on schedule when it comes to making your goals a reality. Having a metric by which to measure your success can keep you motivated during the hard times when it seems like you're not making enough progress. For my part, I return to my business plan time and again to check that I'm acting on my goals.

By setting goals and a deadline for achieving them, you can propel yourself forward through times when you get discouraged. By going back to your guiding document – your business plan – you'll be able to see that you are achieving results, even when it doesn't feel like it. I use a great app called Simpleology — the basic version is free — which helps me with my time management and staying focused on my goals and tasks.

Perhaps more importantly, the planning and goal-setting phase will also help you to develop habits that will make you a success as a self-starter, such as time management, organization, research and analysis.

If you've decided to be more in control of your own future by joining the ranks of the self-employed, the process of coming up with a solid business plan will be an important first test to see if you are suited to being your own boss.

Planning/goal-setting

In this chapter, I will explore why planning and setting short-term and long-range goals is crucial to being an Internet marketer and how this process can help you grow – both as a self-starter and as an individual. Then, I'll share with you some tried-and-tested tips for creating your business plan, from what it will need to include, to how often you should revisit it.

Let's get started!

Why Planning is Crucial to Success as a Self-Starter

If you used to work in a corporate setting or had a boss in your previous job, you may not have been highly involved in the decision-making process that affected the direction of the business.

For employees who work for others, a lack of responsibility has advantages and disadvantages. On the pro list, working within a chain of command means there are lots of people involved in making decisions for the company which means that an individual is unlikely to be responsible for a decision that has a significant effect. But on the cons list, those who work for others don't get the opportunity to take risks that can bring huge rewards.

If making decisions used to be someone else's job, you'll need to change your thinking in order to be a successful Internet marketer.

As your own boss, you will be the one responsible for pushing through setbacks, making time-sensitive choices and responding to changes – not someone else.

It's a daunting prospect, and that's why having a plan to guide you is so crucial.

If you take the time to think through your business goals and what you want to achieve, you will be less intimidated when you face unforeseen complications or need to resolve a situation quickly in order to keep your career on track.

A business plan allows you to define clearly what you intend to achieve. You will discover who your potential clients are, what they need, how to reach them and how to offer value so they become repeat customers.

Planning/goal-setting

Image credit: <a href='http://www.123rf.com/photo_16249911_man-looking-at-business-plan.html'> peshkova / 123RF Stock Photo</a>

While the document will outline your goals in the short-term and long-term, it doesn't have to be a binding document set in stone. In fact, the best business plans will leave room for growth and adjustments as your circumstances change.[1]

In order to create a business plan that will grow with you, you'll need to establish a core foundation – and this exercise can be highly motivating. By distilling your career goals into a mission statement, then charting concrete steps for how to achieve it, you will feel empowered.

---

[1] http://www.thinkbigmagazine.com/business/254-successfully-self-employed Retrieved 27.9.13

Planning/goal-setting

Going through the process of creating a business plan will also help you to develop organizational and financial management skills – and this might be the deciding factor in whether you succeed or fail in Internet marketing.[2]

Self-employed individuals who lack organization waste time and money when they fail to stay on task. Often, they'll have several projects going on at once – and won't be truly focusing on any of them.

If the lack of organization is allowed to continue, they may even jeopardize relationships by failing to communicate on time or risk paying extra fees by not handling the bills on time. The relationships they worked hard to build may flounder if customers are unhappy with the service – which could produce a ripple effect when bad reviews and word-of-mouth are considered.

There are a variety of ways in which lack of organization can hurt the self-employed. Developing good organizational skills is highly important and is one of traits that successful Internet marketers share.

When it comes to being your own boss, "organization" is really another word for "management" – it's not necessarily about having a good filing system or a tidy desk, but whether you have an established approach for effectively handling all of the responsibilities you will need to deal with if you're self-employed.

It all starts with a business plan that outlines what you intend to accomplish and how you will accomplish it by making the most of each workday. Marketing is, of course, crucial to any successful business, but it will never translate into customers and sales without a plan that has been carefully thought out and executed.[3]

Think about it this way: if you had a huge marketing budget at your disposal, would you throw it to the wind by taking out an ad in a publication your target audience doesn't read or by paying for a television or radio spot on a programme that isn't popular among your potential clients?

An effective Internet marketing strategy works in much the same fashion. You don't want traffic from people who are unlikely to contribute to sales, for example. Instead, careful planning of your Internet presence

---

[2] *http://www.entrepreneur.com/article/200730#ixzz2f4BnpqBb* Retrieved 27.9.13

[3] *http://www.articlesbase.com/internet-marketing-articles/why-a-marketing-plan-is-important-in-any-business-619519.html* Retrieved 3.10.13

Planning/goal-setting

will get you to where you want to go.[4] It will outline your objectives. It will create deadlines by which you must achieve certain goals or focus on other tactics. It ensures that customers are satisfied, by carefully evaluating who they are and what they're looking for.[5]

Too many businesses spend large sums on design without having an effective mission statement to guide them about where they should be focusing their marketing efforts. Then the business owners scratch their heads about why they aren't attracting customers.[6]

Key Components of an Internet Marketing Plan

Instead of falling into this trap, I developed key components that my Internet marketing plan needed to include:

- An analysis of the customers I wanted to reach
- The marketing methods that were most likely to reach them
- An evaluation of the competition
- The yardstick I would use to measure whether the tactics were working
- A viable budget for each of my targets.[7]

Without having these components in place, I could have easily floundered. In fact, when it comes to allocating ad money, many businesses are disappointed with the results because they didn't take simple steps to determine who their target audience will be and how they should go about reaching them. Instead, they merely follow the latest trend in Internet marketing with no way of measuring if it is effective for their unique business. They end up wasting money and fading into the background in a crowded field.

Of course, Internet marketing is notorious for being a field where tactics and strategies are constantly changing. Yesterday's tried-and-tested techniques may be obsolete today. That is why you need a well-crafted

---

[4] *http://marketing.about.com/cs/internetstrategy/a/aanetmarketinga.htm* Retrieved 3.10.13

[5] *http://www.articlesbase.com/internet-marketing-articles/why-a-marketing-plan-is-important-in-any-business-619519.html*

[6] *http://www.adaptiveconsultancy.com/strategy/strategy-articles/the-importance-of-a-marketing-plan* Retrieved 3.10.13

[7] Ibid.

Planning/goal-setting

business plan that will allow you to make small tweaks without having to scrap the whole thing.

As a self-employed individual, you will be unlikely to have an unlimited budget. Even if you did, it would be unwise to pour money into unsuccessful strategies, as even the biggest bank accounts can quickly shrink as a result of a series of unwise financial decisions. I have seen many entrepreneurs who thought that start-up money was the answer, when in fact a solid plan was what they were lacking.

Indeed, a business plan will keep you from being one of those who burns brightly for a moment before going out. By going through the process, you'll be on your way to developing a solid reputation.

Put yourself on the road to success with the right approach. The following sections look at the components that every business plan needs.

Details of an Internet Marketing Business Plan

In this section, I will go in more depth into the fundamentals of my online marketing business plan that I shared with you earlier: knowing the audience; finding vehicles to cater to them; evaluating the market; coming up with metrics, and allocating the budget.

1. Know your audience

This is the most important understanding you'll need as an Internet marketer – and one that many established businesses neglect when it comes to developing a marketing strategy. In fact, an audience that is clearly defined and understood can often be the difference when it comes to the success or failure of an online marketing strategy.[8]

Market research firms or focus groups are not necessary for this step. Anyone who is willing to put in the work to find their target market can easily accomplish this task without having to spend money on outsourcing it.

If you know what product or service you intend to sell, finding out who to sell it to is the easy part.[9] It will take time, but you don't need to have previous marketing expertise to accomplish this crucial part of your business plan.

---

[8] *http://www.forbes.com/sites/ilyapozin/2012/06/29/7-tips-for-online-marketing-on-a-tight-budget/* Retrieved 3.10.13

[9] Ibid.

Planning/goal-setting

Often the product itself can guide you when it comes to establishing who is likely to buy it. This process is called creating a "customer profile". Identify them as you would anyone else: what is their age? What is their gender? How much do they have to spend?

Establish who is likely to be interested in your product first before determining how you are going to reach them.

I can't stress this point enough; if your business plan is to start out with the techniques you intend to use before determining who you are trying to reach, you won't have a hope of becoming a success.[10]

Instead, make sure you know your audience **before** you decide on your tactics. Otherwise, you risk putting a lot of time and effort on a road to nowhere.

Other Internet marketers can be shouting from the rooftops about the latest marketing trend all they want; if your customers don't use a particular channel, such as Twitter, you will never be able to sell to them that way.[11] Any Internet marketer who wants to be successful will need to put in the research on their target market first and foremost.[12]

If you're unsure how to define your customer and what your customer profile looks like, follow these simple steps:

- **Describe them in terms of demographics and behaviour.**

Demographics is simple to understand as gender, age and socio-economic status. But psychographics are also important, such as likes and dislikes, personality type, preferences, even hobbies or other interests.[13] Establish what your customers have in common as a starting point. In most cases, there will be several different types of potential customer.

During this process, it may be helpful to create personas for each of the segments of your market. Some business owners find it easy to remember

---

[10] http://www.palmerwebmarketing.com/blog/a-paradox-of-choice-prioritizing-web-marketing-tactics/ Retreived 3.10.13

[11] http://www.forbes.com/sites/ilyapozin/2012/06/29/7-tips-for-online-marketing-on-a-tight-budget/ Retreived 3.10.13

[12] http://www.cybertegic.com/blog/2012/12/the-importance-of-creating-an-internet-marketing-plan/ Retreived 3.10.13

[13] http://www.thewholebraingroup.com/steps-to-creating-an-ideal-customer-profile/ Retreived 3.10.13

Planning/goal-setting

each of their client groups by naming them, keeping written documents of their profile, and even adding pictures of what they might look like.

For example, let's say your product or service appeals to two distinct types of people. Though they share an overlapping interest in what you're selling, they don't have the same personality and they won't necessarily be reachable through the same channels.

In these cases, marketers will often have separate written profiles to remind them of the specific personality types for different potential clients, with names and images – whether it's an image of a real customer or a stock image of what the customer might look like.

"Debbie" might be a stay-at-home mom who enjoys visiting parenting blogs and reading voraciously in her downtime, while "Sam" is a young technophile eager to keep up with the latest trends. Debbie is experienced with managing a household budget and isn't likely to make frivolous purchases for things she doesn't use, while Sam may be a college student or just starting out on a career and may not have a lot of money at his disposal. Adding a name and a picture to the descriptions of these two very different clients will help you remember their unique personality traits and how you might be able to reach them if you're selling something they might both like – such as an e-reader.

Whatever you do, don't lump all your customers into one category. Recognizing that they have unique needs and motivations for buying will allow you to reach out to them as individuals. You'll also be able to anticipate any hesitation they might have in buying from you, and conquer it easily with a targeted message.

- Find out their location.

Now that you can describe the personality and preferences of your ideal customer, find out where they like to hang out. Is it on social media? What types of things do they search for online, and in what search terms? Are they frequent visitors on a particular website or blog?[14]

Assess how your potential customers act both offline and online to get the best understanding of them that you can.

If you know where your customers go, you'll be able to find them – and sell to them. Whether you use this information to pitch a guest blog

---

[14] http://www.convinceandconvert.com/social-media-strategy/how-to-create-customer-profiles-to-reach-your-target-audience/ Retrieved 3.10.13

Planning/goal-setting

post to a website your customers frequent or to craft content they are likely to search for, it will be useful in guiding your online marketing efforts.

- **Find out how they buy.**

In order to know how to market a particular product or service to your customer, you will need to understand the process they go through when making a purchase. Perhaps they have a problem and are looking for a solution to make their lives easier, more efficient or simply more enjoyable. What types of websites do they purchase from? What are their criteria for making a purchase?

Apply what you know about their financial situation as a starting point, then discover what it is about certain products or purchasing processes that appeals to them. This could be ease-of-use or it could be a desire for novelty and innovation. Perhaps they need to visit a website several times before they feel comfortable about making a purchase. Perhaps they are loyal to a particular website but dislike a certain feature. Or perhaps they have no such loyalty and are continuing to look for the best service out there.

By uncovering your potential customers' purchasing habits, you will be able to build relationships with them and cater for them.[15]

- **Reach out to people who fit your ideal customer profile to learn more.**

Sometimes, staying huddled in front of your computer screen conducting market research will mean you are neglecting opportunities to make real connections with the very people you hope to serve. Interviewing people who fit the description of your customers may allow you to gain valuable insights that you never would have uncovered otherwise.

Whether you decide to connect with these clients online or offline, asking them follow-up questions about why they made a certain purchase or why they prefer one company over another can help you gain valuable insight. Perhaps you already know a Sam or a Debbie, or can use your contacts and previous business experience to find them.

I've found that interacting with potential clients helps me learn things I wouldn't otherwise know about them. It can also be the starting point of a relationship with a future customer.

By going through these steps to clearly define your target market, you will be well on your way to a profitable Internet marketing strategy.

[15] *http://www.thewholebraingroup.com/steps-to-creating-an-ideal-customer-profile/* Retrieved 3.10.13

Planning/goal-setting

2. Choose your marketing strategy

Armed with a customer profile and a deep understanding of potential clients, Internet marketers will find it much easier to sort through what techniques they should use to go about reaching them. Suddenly, the endless options available – from PPC to creative content – won't seem so overwhelming. You already know who your customers are, how they make purchases, what search terms they use and what websites they visit.

You'll be glad that you followed my earlier advice to find your market before choosing your method. Now you'll be prepared to cut through the chatter about the latest marketing trends. You will be more likely to garner web traffic that will actually translate into sales instead of blindly racking up page views and visitor numbers from people who are never going to buy what you're selling.

A brief overview of the Internet marketing strategies that may be available to you include:

- Search engine optimization: What search terms do your potential clients use? By researching popular keywords through key online tools, you'll be able to gauge what might work best for your business. It's important to

Image credit: <a href='http://www.123rf.com/photo_15064942_man-touching-virtual-screen-with-seo-process-information-isolated-on-white.html'>bloomua / 123RF Stock Photo</a>

Planning/goal-setting

remember that the top keywords may have a lot of competition, so you'll want to be as specific as possible, all the while keeping your clients' preferences in mind.

- Affiliate marketing: This allows you to earn money through the results of your marketing efforts, and is increasingly a major part of e-retailers' strategies.
- Alliance marketing: By partnering or establishing a relationship with another online business that fits with your product or service, you can offer customers additional value.[16]
- Social media: Twitter, Facebook, Pinterest and other social media sites are ripe for attracting potential customers. Establish which ones your customers prefer so that you can tailor your online presence accordingly. You can use social media to create an identity for your business, to offer unique content for likes and shares, to add another way for customers to get support and to build your reputation.
- Blogging or contributing articles: Creative and unique content that establishes your expertise is increasingly a major factor in search engine rankings. It establishes your credibility in an industry or field. By creating smart content that your customers are looking for and distributing it through appropriate channels, you'll be more likely to get eyeballs – and potential profits. This may involve posting content on your site or pitching it to other sites.
- Webinars or teleseminars: This is another way you can establish yourself as an expert in the field and is becoming increasingly popular. Video marketing typically captures the attention of potential clients for a longer period of time than other types of online marketing efforts.[17] Offering your clients a concrete way to improve their lives or just to hear your name can translate into sales.
- Email marketing: Newsletters that offer content and deals are a direct way to build or enhance relationships with customers.
- Licensing Rights: This is where you purchase the rights to resell the products, usually allowing you to make larger commissions.
- Performance marketing: This could be used to describe a variety of online marketing strategies, such as banner ads, pay-per-click advertising (PPC), pay-per-view advertising (PPV) or pay-per-lead advertising (PPL).

---

[16] *http://internetmarketersgroup.com/2011/02/types-of-internet-marketing-strategies-and-methods/* Retrieved 3.10.2013

[17] *http://internetmarketersgroup.com/2011/02/types-of-internet-marketing-strategies-and-methods/* Retrieved 3.10.2013

Planning/goal-setting

This list is far from comprehensive, as new techniques are emerging and being tested all the time. However, it serves to give you rudimentary knowledge of some of the marketing techniques that are available.

The one you choose will be entirely dependent on your audience. Remember that just because competing sites or services are jumping on the bandwagon of a particular channel doesn't mean that it will work for you.

You also should not get too caught up in trying to become an expert in each online marketing strategy – that could end up being a full-time pursuit that will leave you little time to build your business. Rather, focus on the method that gets you results — which brings us to our next point.

3. Establish benchmarks to chart results

All parts of your planning phase should be created with deadlines for accomplishing tasks and metrics by which to measure the success of your efforts. In my experience, setting a time limit for accomplishing certain goals and creating a means to track my accomplishments offers many benefits – both for my business and for my personal wellbeing. When I feel I'm not seeing the results I want, these benchmarks encourage me by showing what I have accomplished and in how long. It allows me to chart my success in the short-term and the long-term.

It also allows me to avoid wasting time on efforts that aren't going to bear fruit, while focusing my energy on the strategies that are working. Other Internet marketers agree that it is better to focus on getting slight improvements in top performing marketing strategies than to attempt to bring unsuccessful market strategies up to a comparable level of performance.[18]

Measuring Internet marketing efforts with metrics could easily become time-consuming in itself however, and if you spend too much time obsessing over rankings, conversion rates, web traffic or other benchmarks, you may not be spending enough time actually building the parts of your business that will yield results.

That's why some of the deadlines you set should also include how often you measure results. In fact, experts in the field agree that there is almost too much data available to measure, and that Internet marketers

---

[18] *http://www.palmerwebmarketing.com/blog/a-paradox-of-choice-prioritizing-web-marketing-tactics/* Retrieved 3.10.13

Planning/goal-setting

sometimes use the wrong metrics or misinterpret the metrics they have access to.[19]

According to eMarketer CEO Geoff Ramsey, one of the most popular measurements used by Internet marketers today is click-through, also called CTR for click-through rate, but he suggests that many aren't using this metric in the right way. CTR is important, but it shouldn't be the main measurement when gauging the success of online marketing efforts, Ramsey argues.

In fact, there's a term for metrics that really aren't that important and may actually lead Internet marketers in the wrong direction: they're called "vanity metrics".[20] These are the ones that come up in conversation or yield bragging rights – such as the number of Facebook likes for a particular page – but don't translate into something of concrete value for the business owner.

When there is so much information you can monitor, what types of metrics are really important? It will depend on the goals of your particular business. For most, profits are important – but for others, a unique social media identity is more valuable than sales. Whatever your case, don't make the common mistake of "drowning in metrics". Instead, go back to the planning stage of your business to remember your particular goals and pick the measurements that will correlate with your stated objectives.

Although there is a wide range of opinions on what will help Internet marketers prioritize effectively, the following measurements should be part of any business plan:

- Engagement: This involves tracking how long potential customers spend on your site and is a way to demonstrate if you're providing content they see as valuable. The average amount of time on the site should be high. The average pages per visit should also be high. The bounce rate, or people who leave without browsing beyond the home page, should be low. The number of shares on social media sites should also be considered in terms of finding out how valuable visitors find your website, product or service.[21] However, don't become too focused on earning the highest number of Facebook likes or going viral, as smaller businesses will be unlikely to

---

[19] http://blog.hubspot.com/blog/tabid/6307/bid/24226/Top-10-Most-Commonly-Used-Internet-Marketing-Metrics-Data.aspx Retrieved 3.10.13

[20] http://socialmediatoday.com/fixcourse/574771/3-foolish-vanity-metrics-destroy-your-online-marketing Retrieved 3.10.13

[21] http://www.entrepreneur.com/article/224291 Retrieved 3.10.13

Planning/goal-setting

be able to compete with major corporations with endless resources – but that's fine. Instead of total numbers, look at the growth rate and attempt to build your audience through proven practices by a certain number each month, quarter or whatever time frame you establish.

- Source: Where are your customers coming from? How did they find you? You can measure the source of your online traffic in terms of geographic area, search terms or referrals.[22] This is important information for both having a better understanding of your potential clients and figuring out how to target them in the future. You should also look to your backlinks to make sure that websites that point to your site are positive and high-quality. Google's latest algorithm will punish you with lower site rankings if sketchy sites are linking to your website, such as pornographic sites. A metric for your backlink profile will probably need to be a paid service, although you may be able to access rudimentary information through a search engine's Webmaster Tools program.[23]

- Results: This largely refers to the conversion rate, in terms of how many sales are made, how many leads are generated or how popular a certain page or piece of content is among established customers. Google Analytics is a free way to track this benchmark, although paid services are also available. If sales is your top goal, your most important measurement will involve your conversion rate, or how many visitors are actually buying after coming to your site. Perhaps your top priority isn't sales, but popularity, in which case you should be measuring the actions your web visitors take after visiting your site, whether it's through shares, online conversations or some other type of conversion rate that isn't strictly financial.[24]

No matter what metrics you end up choosing, make sure that you continue to focus on your clients, customers or visitors – not on social media popularity or search engines. By all accounts, it is more important to build relationships for repeat views or sales than it is to land higher on a search engine's page. After all, Google isn't the one buying from you, so why would your top priority be satisfying Google instead of actual customers?

4. Know the competition.

Evaluating your competition is just as important as evaluating your potential customers – and just as important for an online business as for a

---

[22] http://blog.hubspot.com/blog/tabid/6307/bid/24226/Top-10-Most-Commonly-Used-Internet-Marketing-Metrics-Data.aspx Retrieved 3.10.13

[23] http://www.entrepreneur.com/article/224291 Retrieved 3.10.13

[24] http://www.entrepreneur.com/article/224291 Retrieved 3.10.13

Planning/goal-setting

bricks-and-mortar business. By finding out who your rivals are, you'll be more likely to create a unique online identity that stands out.[25]

If you neglect this vital aspect of the planning stage, you may never find your potential customers – they'll already be loyal to someone else.

In my opinion, establishing the potential competition should occur before you make a firm decision to jump into any product or service game. I wouldn't want to be one in a sea of many, or not have a way to distinguish myself in a crowded market-place. Potential customers may quickly become overwhelmed by a cacophony of voices vying to be recognized for quality or expertise.[26]

If simple research showed immediately that there was heavy competition in your market, you might do well to consider choosing another product or service to focus on with a niche market – especially if it is your first foray into online marketing. However, if your research instead showed that the business had potential for growth – such as a clear trajectory on Google Trends – then there is an opportunity for you that is ripe for the picking.

Whether you have yet to launch your Internet marketing plans or have already decided what you are going to sell, knowing who your rivals are will guide many other aspects of your strategy. It will help you develop a unique brand identity, gauge customer behaviour, set prices and determine which advertising channels you will use.

Keyword searches, business directories and trade associations are all good starting places for finding out who else is in the field you intend to join. On a local, national or even global scale, you will need to identify how much competition there is and whether the competition you'll be facing is direct or indirect. Direct competitors have the same or similar offerings, while indirect competitors may offer different products or services entirely which could be considered alternatives to what you intend to sell.[27]

The next step is to determine the longevity your competitors have. Search engine rankings often favour domains that have been registered

---

[25] *http://www.internetmarketingpress.com/marketing/evaluating-your-competition/* Retrieved 3.10.13

[26] *http://www.marketingdonut.co.uk/marketing/internet-marketing/ecommerce/how-to-get-the-measure-of-your-competitors* Retrieved 3.10.13

[27] *http://www.internetmarketingpress.com/marketing/evaluating-your-competition/* Retrieved 3.10.13

Planning/goal-setting

first. The free Domain Tools will allow you to determine how long your competitor has had the domain name that is in competition with yours.[28]

Backlinks will also be important to evaluate, as this leads to higher search engine results as well. Establishing how long the competition has been around will give you an idea of their customer base and the advantages they already bring to the table. Though you may never be able to find an exact measure of their site visitors or other metrics, Google Trends can help you evaluate the market potential – which will come in handy when you want to determine how to separate yourself from the competition.

In that vein, take note of the competitors' marketing strategies and look for holes. You might even try this by testing out their products or customer service yourself by placing an order.[29] While browsing competitors' websites, evaluate what is missing. Perhaps they have neglected certain channels that you may be able to leverage to your advantage. There are many ways you can forge a unique identity separate from that of your rivals, from prices to excellent customer service, from creative content to a robust affiliate marketing programme.

You should also seek out what customers are saying about the competitor's business. Perhaps its online reviews leave something to be desired. When you take into account what potential clients are saying, you can offer improvements.[30]

In fact, putting yourself in the shoes of a potential customer is an effective way of both evaluating the competition and coming up with your own goals. Asking yourself simple questions about whether their website is easy to use or looks professional, whether their content is clear, what their presence indicates on Twitter and Facebook or whether they have a search engine optimization strategy that appears to be working will provide insight into what you should do differently.[31]

---

[28] http://www.marketingdonut.co.uk/marketing/internet-marketing/ecommerce/how-to-get-the-measure-of-your-competitors Retrieved 3.10.13

[29] http://www.marketingdonut.co.uk/marketing/marketing-strategy/your-target-market/spotting-gaps-in-your-market Retrieved 3.10.13

[30] http://www.internetmarketingpress.com/marketing/evaluating-your-competition/ Retrieved 3.10.13

[31] http://windingstaircasellc.com/2012/07/internet-marketing-5-areas-to-evaluate-a-competitor/ Retrieved 3.10.13

Planning/goal-setting

Evaluating your competition shouldn't be a one-time-only task. With search engine algorithms constantly changing, innovations being introduced and new products coming to market, regularly checking up on your competition will allow you to stay on top of trends and identify what's missing from the market to use to your advantage.[32]

As an Internet marketer, competition is inevitable. Many are attracted to this growing field who share a passion for innovation, a desire to continue learning and a means to offer value to potential visitors or customers.

I've learned that I can't let potential competition discourage me from pursuing my goals, but I still have to be smart about setting those goals to avoid too much overlap.

5. Set a budget.

The good news about Internet marketing is that you can get started with little to no money down. This may sound like a cheesy sales pitch for used cars, but it's the truth: many Internet marketers have gone on to have lucrative careers without significant start-up costs.[33]

Of course, time is money, and time will be required to devise, implement and monitor strategies necessary for a successful career in this endeavour. Though a limited budget can be used to maximize profits, your own time and what you think it is worth will need to be a consideration.

Not an expert on search engine optimization? Getting the hang of it and monitoring the results are likely to take a significant amount of time. Though it is the best way to increase your visibility and target potential customers, it will certainly involve devoting a certain amount of time and may involve allocating resources to have an outside firm or subscription service implement and monitor the results.[34]

I've found that most successful Internet marketing careers have started with a quality website. Whether you already have one or need to build one, this will be the first area where you need to budget your

---

[32] *http://www.marketingdonut.co.uk/marketing/marketing-strategy/your-target-market/spotting-gaps-in-your-market* 3.10.13

[33] *http://under30ceo.com/how-to-start-an-internet-marketing-business-on-a-budget/* Retrieved 3.10.13

[34] *http://www.forbes.com/sites/ilyapozin/2012/06/29/7-tips-for-online-marketing-on-a-tight-budget/* Retrieved 4.10.13

Planning/goal-setting

time and money. Good design, ease-of-use, content, product pages and a simple purchasing process are the first ingredients you need – well before devising what ways you intend to draw visitors and increase conversion rates.[35] As an online Internet marketer, I am reminded every day that my website is my business – just like a traditional building would be for a local shop. It's the way I separate myself from the competition, attract customers and keep them there for the final sale.

If you have web design experience, then creating your website might be free and easy. If you don't, I would recommend either purchasing online tools that will allow you to create a user-friendly site or hiring a company with a reputation for quality. Whatever avenue you take, keep in mind that your website is the most important aspect of your company. Your first budget consideration should therefore involve purchasing a domain name, buying tools or outsourcing its creation to a professional.

When planning an Internet marketing strategy, the limits of your budget will need to be a consideration. For many, focusing on just one marketing technique and building up expertise in that specific area allows them to keep costs low while effectively selling a product or service.[36]

When going through the steps of creating an Internet marketing plan and setting goals, I'd recommend adding a monetary value to each aspect of your plan. For me, having a firm understanding of my strengths and weaknesses allowed me to break down my budget in terms of tasks I could accomplish on my own versus ones I was likely to outsource.

One of the first steps is to have realistic financial expectations, for both what you already have and what you expect your business to generate on a monthly or quarterly basis. Once you have established an accurate gauge of revenue you are already working with or that you will make, you will need to subtract business expenses – the cost of a home office or of outsourcing tasks, the subscription costs for analytics services or any materials you will need – in order to know how much you can spend on each aspect of your plan.[37]

---

[35] http://fr.slideshare.net/IndiumWebManagement/ive-a-limited-budget-where-should-i-spend-it Retrieved 4.10.13

[36] http://smallbusiness.yahoo.com/advisor/3-internet-marketing-strategies-people-tight-budget-130010805.html Retrieved 4.10.13

[37] http://www.forbes.com/sites/davelavinsky/2013/06/07/three-steps-to-a-solid-marketing-budget/ Retrieved 4.10.13

Planning/goal-setting

Only after you have verifiable figures can you begin breaking it down into budgets. For most Internet marketers, the budget consists almost exclusively of marketing. Potential future expenses or the need for additional employees can often wait, but you may wish to set aside these unexpected costs or growth costs in anticipation.

Affordable Internet marketing strategies offer a wide range of opportunities for getting started, generating traffic and making money without reaching too deep into your funds. This is good news for those with an entrepreneurial spirit but little capital to invest – at least in the initial phase of an Internet marketing plan.

Social media is free to sign up to and use to your advantage, as is content marketing, such as creating articles on a niche area of expertise, blogging on an established platform or pitching ideas to established markets to build up your credibility and get your name out there.

Of course, content marketing will only be free if you do the writing yourself. You'll need to establish if you're a gifted writer who can generate page views and conversations, or else outsource your writing to a qualified individual.[38]

As always, the guide for your budget should match your efforts to reach your target audience. If you are already experienced in an online marketing channel that has worked for you in the past and you know that your customers use it, then you should definitely allocate money to those efforts.

However, you will also need to budget money for untested Internet marketing channels. Set a limited amount at first for the initial phase, as you won't want to waste your limited funds on something that may not work. But conversely, you'll never know if it's the golden ticket unless you try. A small proportion of the marketing costs should be set aside for trying out new venues, without jeopardizing your financial livelihood or your fledgling business.[39]

Just because a particular Internet marketing strategy is free does not necessarily mean that it is the best way to reach potential customers.[40] How-

---

[38] http://smallbusiness.yahoo.com/advisor/3-internet-marketing-strategies-people-tight-budget-130010805.html Retrieved 4.10.13

[39] http://www.forbes.com/sites/davelavinsky/2013/06/07/three-steps-to-a-solid-marketing-budget/ Retrieved 4.10.13

[40] http://www.forbes.com/sites/ilyapozin/2012/06/29/7-tips-for-online-marketing-on-a-tight-budget/ Retrieved 4.10.13

Planning/goal-setting

ever, a host of low-cost options are also available, from affiliate marketing to PPC and email marketing to blogging on your established website.

CHAPTER 4

COACHABILITY

Now that we have examined several traits of the successful Internet marketer, we need to look at another internal attitude that will help you to get the external help you need. That help can come in the form of a person or a website or a book. This attitude is all about learning from others as you grow your business online. I call this vital attitude "coachability".

Coachability is the willingness to learn. Whether you are in the professional arena or the sporting field, you can only advance in your field if you are able to continually learn. In the context of personal improvement, your coachability quotient refers to how much you can learn from others without letting restraints like your ego hold you back from assimilating information. You can only learn and improve yourself if you are coachable.

Even Internet marketers who have made a lot of money say that they still have much to learn. That willingness to learn largely explains their ability to make a nice profit consistently. The best marketers know that there is always something out there that they can benefit from, sources of knowledge that will help them. We will look at some of these sources and hear from some of these marketers in this chapter.

This trait is not something that can be learnt from books and classes. Instead, coachability is gained through a change in perspective, or a change in heart. Those who are naturally coachable usually have certain personality traits or characteristics that make them malleable and open-minded. Open-mindedness is important in order to receive any kind of information without bias and to learn from it, as is the ability to listen with the intent to learn. But there are five specific traits that can make a difference to how well you receive knowledge from trainers.

Coachability

Coachability traits

1. **Faith:** Probably the most important asset that a coachable individual can have is faith in the coach. It can be difficult sometimes to overcome our egos and stoop to the role of pupil, but this false pride can be even more fatal to progress than an incompetent teacher. Therefore it is always important to have faith in the coach, though this doesn't mean that prospective teachers should not be screened to find the best-suited mentor.

2. **Humility:** In order to have faith in another person, humility is necessary. Humility teaches us that there are things we need a teacher for, as there are things we cannot do on our own. It induces us to bring about a positive change in our behaviour and be more receptive to the experiences and wisdom of others.

3. **A willingness to act:** Without determination to learn, and positive action on our part, we cannot expect to find the right teacher for us. Therefore coachability demands an action bias.

4. **Disinterested sense of purpose:** Pure knowledge evades those who seek it with selfish interests. Seeking wisdom for the sake of wisdom is the purpose that a coachable individual needs to have. If making money through that knowledge or using the teacher as a launch pad for one's career is the goal, then there are impure conditions being attached to the training. This cannot result in true receptiveness to the knowledge imparted by the teacher.

5. **Willingness to give up control:** Finally, a coachable person is one who is willing to forsake control for the sake of knowledge. Often, we unknowingly put our mentors in difficult positions by expecting results in exchange for control. In other words, we place constraints on our relationship with our mentors, leading to closed-mindedness. Learning to give up control without the expectation of results is one of the first steps to gaining productive wisdom.

Coachability demands a suppression of the ego and a lowering of defences. Pride and ego are the biggest obstacles to learning and they must be completely suppressed in order for wisdom to enter. The best professionals in their respective fields are those who are aware that they need coaching, and accept it with humility.

Let me dig a little deeper into each of the five traits listed above.

Coachability

Image credit: <a href='http://www.123rf.com/photo_19870137_helping-hand-word-cloud--coaching-concept.html'>grasycho / 123RF Stock Photo</a>

Coach or Mentor?

If you are going to have the type of faith in your coach that you need to succeed, then you need to be very careful about which coach you choose to learn from. By the way, there is hot debate in the marketing field, and in the entrepreneurship domain in general, over whether a newcomer needs a "coach" or a "mentor". Depending on how you define the words, I would recommend a "coach" in some cases and a "mentor" in others. I think my idea of the word "coach" blends the definition of these two concepts well.

In short, some writers say that coaches are people that you hire on a temporary basis, and then those coaches set you free. There is no sense of a long-term relationship with a coach. I'm not sure that is correct, but if it is, then I would probably lean towards the idea of a mentor.

Coachability

In many of the popular writings today, mentors are considered to be people who stick with you for the lifetime of your business. These people are often not paid, but they are people that you attach yourself to in order to glean all of the wisdom that they have in a particular field.

My aim in this chapter is not to have an extended debate over what a coach is and what a mentor is. My point is that you need to be a learner, and often that learning is best accomplished as you sit at the feet of a successful marketer. If you find someone that you really like and have to pay for his/her services, then I guess you would call that person a coach, and a temporary one at that. That might work best for you. Perhaps you could check in with that coach from time to time for years to come. That would make them more of a mentor, according to popular literature.

If you find someone that you want to learn from, and practise this on a more informal basis, then you would probably have to call that person a mentor. You might meet this sort of mentor at a professional gathering, or perhaps come across him/her online. If you check in with this person on a regular basis for many years, with no money exchanging hands, then you should probably call this person a mentor.

It doesn't really matter what you call the person that you are learning from. The point is that you humble yourself enough to learn well, and you realize that you absolutely need the knowledge of others. Whether it's a coach or mentor, just find someone to learn from.

Coaching vs. Mentoring

To help understand the difference between how these terms are used in many places on the Net, the following table examines the pros and cons of coaches versus mentors:

Coach	Mentor
Contact usually done by phone or email	Contact usually done by phone or in person
Sessions usually run 15-30 minutes	Time together can be from one hour to a half-day
Coach makes suggestions, usually in a generalized fashion, such as "make this paragraph more compelling".	Mentor more likely to get his/her hands dirty and do actual work as well as explain the thought process behind the changes s/he makes.

Coachability

Coach does not do the actual work for you.	An example would be "Here is a similar paragraph I wrote for a recent campaign that worked."
Paid by the session	Might not be paid at all. If paid, and hired by you, usually given a monthly retainer fee in addition to percentage of increase in sales revenue.
Usually come out of networks and make $15-$30/hour	Can command rates from $200-$2,000/hour
Has an agenda for each session, with assigned tasks	Often will take the time to dream with you and serve as a sounding board

This table has been adapted from one that was used to argue for a mentor over a coach.[1] I would lean towards the mentor as described in this table, but I think the terms can be almost interchangeable.

If you have a very limited budget, then you might want to try out a coach for a few sessions and see if his/her feedback and guidance is valuable. The best route to go is to actively seek out a mentor who will give you some of their time at no cost. This mentor-mentee relationship could grow into an actual friendship. If you do pursue this type of person, be sure to let him/her know how much you appreciate their time and effort. You could take your mentor to lunch or dinner on a regular basis, and perhaps even publicize their work as you build your career. Use common sense in honouring your mentor, and don't take advantage of the kindness shown to you.

If you have a large budget and know for certain that a prospective mentor is foolproof and always gets results, then you should consider paying big money to glean some of that wisdom. Again, my point is that none of us know it all and we all need to learn from others in the field, especially those who have been at it longer than we have.

---

[1] *http://herenextyear.com/internet-marketing-mentoring-versus-coaching.php*, retrieved 6.10.13

Coachability

How to Best Choose a Coach/Mentor

So how do you find someone who is worth learning from; someone who has done well in Internet marketing and is gifted at communicating what they have learned along the way?

Here are a few steps to get you started on your quest to find a great coach/mentor:[2]

1. Do a search of the latest research.

Don't restrict your quest simply to websites. Some of them can claim just about anything. Look around on YouTube, check the presenters' credentials, and watch some videos that might summarize much of what you need in just a few minutes.

You should also take a trip to your local library or bookstore. We should never get so modern that we forget the value of a good book. Look around on Amazon and see which authors come highly recommended. You might be able to find a $10 book that will give you many of the insights that you need, and that book could save you hours and hours of time floating around the Web looking for wisdom.

Being an Internet marketer, you should also take an extended look at the most recommended blogs. There are some outstanding blogs out there relating to our field. Find a few that you like and follow them. Some of these blogs have long, long lists of Internet marketers that you can pursue.

As you are looking around at these books, blogs and sites, you could very well find a potential coach/mentor or two. You probably do not want to try and get a millionaire marketer's time for free, but it doesn't hurt to ask!

You'll probably want to find a mid-level marketer who strikes you as having a lot of good ideas and insight in the field. Often these marketers will offer coaching for a fee, or at least a set of files or videos that expand on their ideas. If you have the funds available, you might want to put down a fee to get more access to someone you and others perceive to be a true guru.

Another tack, however, would be to contact someone who is an acknowledged expert, and propose weekly or monthly interactions, by

---

[2] *http://www.wikihow.com/Find-an-Internet-Marketing-Mentor*, retrieved 6.10.13

Coachability

email, phone or Skype. These experts will be very busy people, but you might be able to find one who can give you 30 minutes every two weeks, for instance. That might be just the boost that you need to get your own business up and thriving.

I would also recommend a more organic way to find a mentor/coach. Meet with other professionals in your city, if at all possible, and find one that seems to know what s/he is doing. You can meet with them regularly to pick their brains and get clarity on what you need to do to succeed in this field.

However you choose to pursue a mentor/coach, do find one!

2. Decide how much you can pay for coaching/mentoring.

As stated earlier, it is indeed possible to find a mentor who will not charge you for their time. That does still happen in this world, believe it or not.

However, in many cases, you will run across prospective coaches who charge a standard fee. Before you get too far in your search for a coach, decide how much you are willing to pay to get coaching. Take a look at your business plan and see what you have in the budget for personal research and development. Choose your mentor/coach according to what you have available in the budget. Don't become too discouraged if you do not have four figures to spend on mentoring. You might get all that you need from a $250 video set and booklet. You could even get all that you need from a $10 book and a new friend that you meet at a marketing conference.

How do you spend money typically? Do you make large outlays without much thought? If so, then you will be more likely to hire a coach/mentor for $200/hour. If you are living on a budget then you might want to start slowly with your investment in this area and see how it goes. You can glean a lot of good advice from free sites, buy a book or two and latch on to someone who's been at it a little longer than you have at your city's next young businesspersons' club meeting, for example.

3. Join an association.

Speaking of clubs, look around for a local, national or international marketing association that you can join. It would be best to find such an organization that has local chapter meetings that you could attend.

Coachability

At such meetings, your chances of finding a potential mentor/coach are far higher than if you simply drop in on your city's young professionals' happy hour. The fees for these associations are not unreasonable. Join one to expand your network of contacts and boost your chances of finding a coach/mentor.

4. Apply for an internship.

Like most internships these days, many of the ones that you can find working for an Internet marketer will be unpaid. Don't be too quick to discount their value, though. If you can give several hours a day or week to learning from a pro in this way, then pursue it by all means. You might not intern with the most successful marketer in the world, but you'll learn a lot by watching how they go about their business. You can learn not only positive lessons, but also what to avoid as you build your own business.

Many marketers will respond to a simple email inquiry. Give it a try if you spot one in your area, or if you can intern online. CareerBuilder and Craigslist, among others, will list many possibilities for these types of internships.

5. Hire a consultant.

This could possibly lead to a coach/mentor-type relationship, or it may not. You can go in with the idea that it will be a short-term relationship, and if it turns out to be more than that, you can be pleasantly surprised.

Even if it is just short-term, you can gain a lot from a skilled consultant who makes his/her living giving pointers to newbies like yourself.

Many of these consultants will do group sessions, so if you can find a few other friends that also need some counsel, you might be able to get a top-notch consultant at a great price.

If you have the money available for a one-to-one session with a consultant, that could be even better. Sometimes the advantage of having one person to interact with is well worth the money. You can tailor the session(s) to your specific needs and get all of your questions answered in a short space of time. This is in contrast to a group setting, where the consultant has to answer all of the participants' questions, and you sit there twiddling your thumbs while the consultant spends time on issues that you don't need advice on. In other words, the higher price for a one-to-one session could be worth it for you.

6. *Thoroughly vet your choice of coach/mentor.*

Any potential mentor should have evidence of success in the field. Otherwise, s/he is not worth your time. Ask to have a look at a list of clients, so that you can inquire about how the mentor has helped them in their businesses. If at all possible, try to find out actual income that the prospective coach has made in the past few years.

The Web can be very helpful here. See if there are reviews of your potential coach/mentor online. Keep in mind that few mentors have unanimously positive reviews. However, you should be able to tell from the tone of the reviews if the coach/mentor uses up-to-date materials and is current in the field.

Be a Lifelong Learner

Please do not think for a moment that enlisting a coach/mentor is the only way to learn about how to become a successful Internet marketer. Far from it!

"Coachability" does not just mean that you are willing to sit at the feet of a given guru and lap up anything that s/he dispenses. No, there are many other ways to be coachable, and many other ways to learn. You need to take advantage of all of them.

Much of this book (perhaps to your disappointment, perhaps to your delight) is about attitude, and that is what I want to zero in on in this chapter as well. Being coachable is an attitude. It is the idea that you not only don't know it all, you will NEVER know it all.

Because of that, there is always something to learn, especially in a field like ours, which changes quickly as new algorithms are invented, the variety of social media expands and new training on selling emerges. Our field changes at lightning speed. Don't be afraid of that. Instead, do your best to keep up, as best as a human being can.

You can't devour all of the information and knowledge that is out there. No one can! But, you can try your best to take advantage of the galaxy of information that is available and use what you find to be helpful.

Coachability

When top Internet marketers are polled about what they believe are the keys to their success, they almost always point to an attitude of being a lifelong learner. This good advice applies to any occupation, obviously, but it might be even more important for us Internet marketers, given how rapidly our field evolves.

As was noted in the article "Top 10 Qualities of an Internet Marketer":

> Internet marketing changes very fast, because of the sheer size of the industry things change literally overnight. So you must have a passion for lifelong learning. If you ever think that you have learnt enough and now you don't need to learn, trust me, you'll be outdated before you can even complete that thought of yours. 'Keep learning and keep growing' is the motto of this industry.[3]

I couldn't agree more! Especially with the line that says, "you'll be outdated before you can even complete that thought of yours."

John Jantsch of Duct Tape Marketing puts it this way:

> I consider "curiosity" to be my superpower. I have to know how things work and why. It's a trait that drives my wife crazy from time to time but it also drives me to experiment, try new things, read deeply in fields unrelated to marketing and think beyond the obvious — all of these things I believe make me a better marketer or at least allow me to provide more value to my community.[4]

I love this quote because it raises the valuable point that not all of the expertise you will need is to be found only on blogs and in books by Internet marketers. Have a look around at other successful businesspeople, other entrepreneurs, other leaders and find out what you can learn from them.

---

[3] http://qadirmemon.com/top-10-qualities-of-an-internet-marketer/

[4] http://www.entrepreneur.com/article/228059#ixzz2f48rGnsk

Coachability

Image credit: <a href='http://www.123rf.com/photo_18917880_businesswoman-with-a-big-question-mark.html'>alphaspirit / 123RF Stock Photo</a>

Also, think about how curiosity could apply to you. Are you willing to simply implement a new technological process in your business without fully understanding how it works? That might serve you well for a while, but those who insist on understanding *how* a new social media operates will often utilize it better in the long run.

Don't miss the connection between risk-taking and curiosity either. In reading about how other entrepreneurs make their way in the business world, you might want to borrow ideas from them and apply them to Internet marketing. Who knows what that sort of mash-up will bring? Risk-taking is a valuable trait for an entrepreneur, and curiosity tends to feed that instinct. "I wonder if face-to-face meetings will help my relationship with local clients." "I wonder if (fill in the blank)". This is how new advances

Coachability

are made in any industry, Internet marketing included. Ask "what if" a lot, and you will find that many of those questions arise out of your curiosity and investigations into other fields and businesses.

Adam Kleinberg of Traction echoes this theme:

> I never stop learning. I've accomplished a few things: I've run an agency for 12 years; worked with some of the world's greatest brands; my company just came in second place on the West Coast for Ad Age Small Agency of the Year. You'd think I would consider myself a guy who knows what he's doing. But I don't. I walk into my office every day asking, "How could I do this better?" I take every opportunity I can to learn the answer to that question. I'm like a sponge when I meet people, trying to soak up bits of their knowledge. I read voraciously. I attend conferences. I watch people. I experiment. We live in such a rapidly changing world — the only way to constantly improve as a marketer is to seek out lessons to learn, each and every day.[5]

Did you read that quote closely? Someone who has experienced great success says, "I walk into my office every day asking, 'How could I do this better?'" That should stun you and inspire you to cultivate curiosity in your own life. If someone who has had a nice run of prosperity constantly asks how he can do things better, then you should, too.

The response to his own question is also instructive: "I take every opportunity I can to learn the answer to that question. I'm like a sponge when I meet people, trying to soak up bits of their knowledge. I read voraciously. I attend conferences. I watch people. I experiment."

Does this describe you? Or are you the type of person who believes "I don't need anyone's help. I'm smart. I can figure this out on my own."

Now we are back to what I mentioned earlier in the chapter. You are going to need a humble and teachable attitude if you are to be a successful Internet marketer. If someone from an award-winning firm says that he can never learn enough, then who are you to say that you cannot learn from anyone?

Are you like Kleinberg, or are you threatened by other marketers? When you do attend a conference, do you room alone and skip some of

---

[5] *http://www.entrepreneur.com/article/228059#ixzz2f49Zuuee*

Coachability

the seminars to sightsee and sleep, or do you attend all that you can and meet as many people as possible? You know precisely what I am talking about: the difference between a teachable person and an arrogant one that does not want to learn.

Note again in this quote the direct relationship between curiosity and risk-taking. Kleinberg says that he watches people then experiments. You should be doing the same. Watch what others are doing, in many fields, and seek to apply their wisdom to your marketing. See what happens.

I cannot promise you that you will become a marketing expert if you rise to this level of daily curiosity, but I can tell you that any successful Internet marketer will be coachable and wanting to learn all they can, all the time. Even though Internet marketing does seem to attract a high percentage of lone wolves who want to work at home and not be around people, it does not mean that you have to isolate yourself and not seek out all the knowledge that you can.

Sure, you can learn a lot through books, but I find that people, actual human beings, are my best source of information and wisdom as I build my business. Don't stand in the corner at the next professional happy hour! Mingle and think of yourself as a sponge.

As was noted in an earlier chapter, a fantastic source of inspiration and know-how are other entrepreneurs. Joanna Lord of BigDoor testifies to this person-to-person mining of knowledge:

> I make time to meet with start-up founders. We all get super busy but I do a couple of coffees or chats a week with new founders whether in person or via email. They tend to be tackling new market problems which keeps my creative juices flowing, and their passion is contagious. When I approach a new marketing campaign or channel or challenges I try to keep in mind smart people are out there hustling to build great things and I find I push myself for the better.[6]

I appreciate this quote because it ties together many of the themes of this book. It proves that if you are coachable, you will have your motivation replenished as you are inadvertently "pushed" to work harder and smarter. As Lord puts it, her contact with other start-up founders "keeps my creative juices flowing, and their passion is contagious." Indeed.

---

[6] Ibid.

Coachability

Invest in Yourself

Perhaps if I've discussed coachability in more depth than you thought possible, you will have had this thought: "This all sounds great, but I do not have the time or money to be curious."

I understand this reaction. None of us have the time or money to fritter either away. You will need to change a fundamental idea about your own value and how to build a successful Internet marketing business. You will have to see YOURSELF as a valuable asset, not just the latest website tools or communication outlet. You spend willingly on those, but how often do you spend money on yourself?

Don't pat yourself on the back too hard for being someone who never spends any money on themself, especially in the early days of your enterprise. Bravo if you have forgone that luxury automobile or expensive pair of shoes until you hit a certain profit margin. However, this investment in yourself must begin from the early days and be maintained throughout your career. I am telling you that you are worth it, and that you need to invest in yourself to stay abreast of all that is happening in our field.

The entrepreneurs who have risen to the top of our field ALL[7]:

- buy and read business and marketing books
- subscribe to magazines that are relevant to the task
- digest reports, journals and newsletters that help them
- scan websites and industry publications for new bits of knowledge
- join business associations and clubs
- attend business and marketing seminars, workshops and training courses (even if they have mastered a particular area, by the way)
- understand that there is ALWAYS a way to do business better, in less time, with less effort
- never stop investing in themselves

I will close with one final powerful quote from the article "Six Most Important Qualities of a Successful Internet Marketer". In this article, Mitch Hell notes that the first essential trait to succeed online is the one I have spent an entire chapter talking about: coachability. He says that

---

[7] http://www.entrepreneur.com/article/200730#ixzz2f4BHa3Cl

Coachability

successful affiliate marketers have a high willingness to learn and to be trained to succeed:

> The Internet is always changing and there are always new things popping up every day. If someone would have placed an ad on the Internet in the early days of the Internet they would have been a multi-millionaire by now. Times have changed now and the way you sell and market on the Internet has changed also. That means you must spend time and money educating yourself to the fullest if you want to get to the top as fast as you can. We advise that you read books, research and even get a coach to help you learn the ropes if you are just starting. If you are experienced, you know just as we do that you always have ongoing learning to do. So, get educated and NEVER stop learning or you WILL fall behind.[8]

---

[8] *http://online-money-today.com/6-important-qualities-of-a-successful-internet-marketer/*

CHAPTER 5

ATTITUDE

Now that I have covered desire, motivation, planning and coachability, it is time to explore a necessary trait that overlaps with many of the previous topics, but can also stand alone as well. Perhaps this chapter needs a plural noun, because you will need a variety of attitudes from a diversity of sources to make it as an Internet marketer.

Drawing on thoughts from many successful Internet marketers and other entrepreneurs, I will summarize the types of attitude that you will need to persist and succeed in e-commerce which can be broken down into:

- Attitudes towards your work in general
- Attitudes towards yourself

In addition, I want to explore more generally the importance of a positive attitude and how that will impact your life and business.

I want to look more carefully at both of these key areas of attitude and to highlight a few articles on attitude in general that I think are worth mentioning.

Attitudes Towards Your Work

We begin with your attitudes towards your work, specifically as an Internet marketer. As you have taken the risk to bid "adieu" to your 9-to-5 job in that big office building populated by tiny cubicles, you will need an entirely new set of attitudes to succeed on your own. Have you stopped to think about that?

Having attitudes such as "I hate this place", "I don't care how well this company does as long as I get my holiday bonus", "I couldn't care less about the other departments", "I can't wait to go home", "I wish the weekend were here already" and so on, have NO place in the life of an Internet marketer.

At the other end of the spectrum, you mustn't take yourself too seriously as you try to make a living on the Web. Perhaps you have come from a job where there were huge responsibilities and you felt like the future of the civilized world rested on your shoulders. You can forget that, too, as you dive into Internet marketing.

As D.J. Waldow, the founder and CEO of Waldow Social puts it:

> I remind myself: Nobody dies in marketing. Marketers are not doctors. We are not in jobs where people's lives are in our hands. We are helping businesses solve problems, reduce costs and/or make more money. My advice: Have fun. Smile. Laugh. Dance. Don't take yourself too seriously. Be human. Positive energy is contagious - SPREAD IT![1]

I greatly appreciate this sentiment and I need to remind myself of it from time to time. It can be quite easy to get caught up in the apparent seriousness of all that we do as Internet marketers. We are on our own; we have no life-raft if the ship sinks. We make as much money as we earn each day. No one is giving us a regular wage, in most cases. If we get distracted or ill, we will probably lose money.

In that atmosphere one can get very anxious and take one's job much too seriously. It's a great reminder that we are not in the healthcare industry, for instance, so no one's life is at stake as we do keyword research or blog about something we've learned. We are not soldiers on the battlefield, either, eluding bullets and firing rockets at enemies, in a place where people do die.

No, we are marketers, and we are trying to help people sell products. That is a noble calling but it will not determine the future of the planet, in most cases. If you have an account that is campaigning for green living, then perhaps you could say that you are saving the planet every day, but for the most part we must remember to smile and laugh and not take ourselves too seriously as we build our businesses.

---

[1] *http://www.entrepreneur.com/article/228059#ixzz2f49AjLNW*

Attitude

Image credit: <a href='http://www.123rf.com/photo_18461593_happy-businesswoman-with-laptop-and-isolated-on-white.html'>tomwang / 123RF Stock Photo</a>

As for dancing on the job, if you need a break to move around, then go ahead and take one in any way that you see fit, though I do not recommend dancing while interacting with clients or verifying your accounts receivable!

At the same time that we are rejoicing over the ability to work from home and actually make a decent living from it, we should also have the attitude that we are not going to get too comfortable with our routine and profits. Rather, we need to make a conscious effort to push ourselves out of our comfort zone to explore new areas and remain stimulated. I like the brief ditty: keep it fresh.

Brian Honigman, a phenomenal content marketing consultant, agrees:

> I constantly experiment with new ideas, platforms, technologies, companies and people to see what's working or what could potentially work for the future. Applying this practice to everything I do helps to consistently push me out of my comfort

Attitude

zone, make me more agile and flexible to the needs of customers and partners.[2]

I appreciate the verb "push" in this quote because, as discussed in earlier chapters, much of your motivation will have to come from within. This means that the push to get out of your comfort zone will likewise have to come from inside you.

As part of that pushing, you might need to remind yourself that what you are embarking on is constructing a business, not just indulging in a pastime when you feel like it. Even though you have broken free from the tentacles of the corporate world, you should not treat your Internet marketing business as a hobby or sideline.

I have found that this can be a strong temptation for many new marketers, especially those who have hit rough waters for a while and perhaps have back-up savings or capital to rescue them. They can get discouraged and put less effort into their business, at a time when they should be doing the opposite.

One of the oldest Internet marketing forums on the Web, called Warrior Forum, has a few bloggers that I like. These men and women skip the fancy talk and technical jargon and get right to the point. There is one post I particularly liked on this subject, about how to treat your personal enterprise, having an attitude of seriousness while not taking yourself too seriously. That balance is indeed possible, and I'd like to think that I prove it every day.

Here is the extended quote that I want to share with you:[3]

> You might not have the "right" attitude. What I mean is this: If you have decided to do this as a second income, or a full time job altogether, great. But, you need to understand that this is a "business" and you need to treat it as such. It is entirely up to you how much you build this up. You see, it is not just about throwing up a site, and saying okay I'm going to be a millionaire now....wrong!

---

[2]   http://www.entrepreneur.com/article/228059#ixzz2f49AjLNW

[3]   http://www.warriorforum.com/blogs/trevor75/13703-proper-attitude-internet-marketing.html, retrieved 27.9.13.

Attitude

Believe me I know what I'm talking about, because I fell into the same trap. I thought I could just throw up a simple credit card site, and have droves of people just start flooding to my site. However, some of you might be getting frustrated because you have had a site for three months now, and are not making any money yet. Well that is most likely because you are not treating this as your business. You need to apply the same attitude, and tactics, that you would if you did own a proper business.

Understand this, that a lot of companies do not even show a profit their first year. Do not pay any attention to the gurus who say you can make $50,000 in 45 days, hogwash! Sure they can do it, because they have an email list of 35,000 people and have spent time building up their business for the last 10 years. You probably have not done that, or had time to, yet. Treat it like your own child and it will make you proud, I promise.

I think that it is most valuable to hear from real Internet marketers out there in the trenches making a living, rather than from so-called experts who might teach at a school or are still living off an inheritance.

This excellent blog post has several outstanding points about the type of attitude you need towards your business:

1. Ultimately, the success or failure of your business will come down to you. Sure, you can blame a sluggish economy for some of your struggles, but what you put into your business will shape what you get out of it, every time. So, your attitude needs to be that it is a business for you, not a phase of life or something you "do on the side". Own up to it and tell people proudly, "I'm an Internet marketer, full time." This attitude of yourself as a business owner will help you greatly.

2. Business will not come to you; you will need to go out and get it. The Internet is not a magical slot machine, as if you can buy a domain name, slap up a primitive site and wait for the currency to begin to roll in. Far from it. You will need to imagine yourself in a storefront office in your town. If you simply sit in that room and wait for everyone in the community to discover you, you will soon be growing cobwebs from your nose to your desk. You need to go out and make yourself known, make an effort to build your enterprise, and the results will come. Remember: storefront.

3. Other "marketers" will make all sorts of claims about how much money they made and you should make. Don't pay any attention to those inflated and imaginary figures. Instead, plug away and watch how your profits

grow as you persist in hard work. I love the image of your business being a "baby". You will need to raise it with patience and a vision for the future. Treat it well and it will be good to you.

Attitudes Towards Yourself

Now I move on to the all-important attitudes towards yourself. This is a very important area and one that is not discussed often enough, in my opinion. What I want to know is, how do you <u>really</u> feel about yourself? Do you see yourself as a failure because you did not advance as quickly as you would have liked in the corporate world? Do you hear voices from long ago when people told you that you were not very smart or talented? Perhaps you were raised by parents who did not affirm you often or enough.

I do not want to play pop psychologist, not even for a moment, but I want you to take a deep look inside and tell me how you see yourself. What do you think when you first look in the mirror in the morning? What do you think at noon when you are already a little tired and want to shut your laptop for the day? What do you think when you do not get the contract that you bid for?

As you look inside for a few moments, I want you to realize that you might need to do some serious attitude correction if you hope to make it as an Internet marketer. That's right: I said that you can know all the tricks of the trade and apply 90% of this book to your venture, but if you do not have a deep-down belief in yourself, it could all go awry. You might just quit too soon, before the profits roll in at a reasonable rate and you make an actual living at this.

I again quote from the article "The 10 Essential Qualities of an Internet Marketer":[4]

> A successful Internet Marketer believes in his success. The reality is actually way more powerful than this: "For a successful Internet marketer, failure is not an option!" Does this mean that everything runs smoothly and perfectly the first time around for those successful persons? Not at all! Most (if not all) Internet millionaires encountered multiple set-backs. Their strength comes from the fact that they took these set-backs merely as challenges and got more motivated from them[…]Honestly evaluate if you truly believe in yourself and your success. Are you putting up

---

[4] http://birdherd.com/the-10-essential-qualities-of-a-successful-internet-marketer/

excuses? Do you often catch yourself downtalking about your own goals?

I appreciate this quote on so many levels. Failure is indeed not an option if you have begun your own marketing business. This means that you will rebound after set-backs because you believe in yourself to such a high degree that you view these temporary obstacles as mere challenges. Rather than demotivating you, they will motivate you.

I also like the link between belief in self and belief in success. If you don't believe deep down that you are smart enough to master what needs to be done to make your business work, then you will be continually discouraged and much more prone to laziness, I assure you.

Image credit: <a href='http://www.123rf.com/photo_13725707_a-construction-barrier-with-the-words-this-challenge-brings-you-one-step-closer-to-success-to-motiva.html'>iqoncept / 123RF Stock Photo</a>

If, however, you have a rock-solid belief in yourself, then you will not be shaken by challenges; rather you will draw on past successes and say, "I overcame something like this before, I will do it again."

From another excellent site with blog posts about making it as an Internet marketer come these thoughts on the concept of self-belief:[5]

---

[5] http://bigideamakesmoney.com/successful-internet-marketing-business-attitude/, retrieved 3.10.13

Attitude

> When it comes to the Internet Marketing business, you need to have the right mental point of "you". Think that there is a solution to every problem. Be exploratory and never stop asking questions to other marketers or to Google. Therefore, never stop exploring, there is a solution to every problem!
>
> Be patient. Real internet marketers are patient people, because they know that their efforts will pay off sooner or later.

This post also brings up several areas of attitude towards self that I endorse. I appreciate the phrase "the right mental point of you"! That is absolutely correct, but the blog poster went further, to illustrate what this proper perspective will look like in your everyday attitudes as you persist towards your goals.

If you have the right view of you, you will believe that there are solutions, not just problems, and that you will find those solutions, given enough time. This is incredibly important to your business success. If all you see is a problem and do not believe that you are clever enough to find the solution, then you will be tempted to give up on many occasions.

Likewise, being patient is related to self-belief because if you have a profound belief in yourself, you will think that it is only a matter of time before your hard work begins to pay off and you will learn the ropes to become a success. People who do not have this sort of self-belief can panic easily if there are set-backs. They can lose confidence and either radically modify their original plan or discard it altogether. Your self-belief, I believe, will be key to you maintaining the patience that you need to be a long-term success.

The Importance of a Positive Attitude

I will take this occasion to repeat what I said in an earlier chapter: there may or may not be merit in belief in the "law of attraction" that you can visualize something and make it happen but I do not believe in visualizing without action. You are free to believe in this New Age concept but that is not the point of this section or of this book.

However, I do believe in the power of positive attitude. I believe in it not simply because I have seen its power again and again in my personal

Attitude

and professional life, but also because many others in our business see it as foundational to persevering in a challenging business.

Sanne Berrig, an extremely well-respected Internet marketer, blogs regularly about what she believes are the keys to achieving a strong level of achievement in the field. She wrote this about the importance of attitude:

> Your attitude is vital to your business success. In fact, I would almost say it's even more important than learning the skills. Obviously, you need to learn the nuts and bolts of your business – how to write a blog post, how to market that blog post, how to build your email list, and develop a relationship with those on your list, etc. But without the right attitude, these things are just tools lying unused in the tool shed. The attitude is what will help you put those tools to work.[6]

I admire the way that she phrases the relationship of technique to attitude. You can't major on one without the other. Both are essential. Yet it would be wrong to believe that mastering techniques will be the ultimate formula for your success in Internet marketing. A proper attitude must accompany the learning of those techniques.

Berrig goes on to describe the multi-faceted attitude that the successful Internet marketer needs to have:

> **Understand Your Purpose** – What was the reason that made you feel so alive when you started your home business? Maybe it was to create a financially secure future for yourself and your family, or to finally be debt-free. Maybe you wanted more time off. Get really clear on your reason and keep it in the forefront of your business every day. This is called knowing your "Why".
>
> **Be Coachable** – Assuming that you already know everything will cause you to fail quicker than anything else. You need to stay open and coachable. Remember that others have gone before you, using the same system, and have become wildly successful.

---

[6] http://www.pureleverage.com/sanneberrig/having-the-right-attitude-for-success/, retrieved 5.10.13.

Attitude

Stay Positive – Like anything else, there will be ups and downs along the way. Staying positive will help you achieve success, but will also make the journey more enjoyable along the way. There are a lot of things in your business that you don't have control over. You can't control whether people join your business and you can't control your company's compensation plan, but you can always change your attitude.

With the proper attitude, you will be able to remember how much sense the business made when you first started. There will be no room for discouragement in your business. Instead, you'll say, "I know why I joined the business, I know what I'm doing now, and I'm confident in where I'm going. No one will derail me because I am too focused on my objective."[7]

There is much to unpack from this passage, some of which re-emphasizes points that I made earlier in this book.

Let's begin with the understanding of your purpose as you form a positive attitude. Your mind-set in starting an Internet business is not as simply an escape from drudgery but a launch into an adventure, full of risks and rewards. If you are only focusing on the escape *from* somewhere or something, then you will have difficulty maintaining a positive attitude. Notice Berrig's phrasing as she describes how she views her purpose, and answers the critical question of "Why".

She mentions goals such as living debt-free, financial security, additional time off and providing for your family. These are all powerful components of the "Why" that you should be able to formulate. Keep that "Why" positive and you will have the right mind-set every day when you hit the 'on' button and settle down to work.

If it helps to make a small card listing your "Why" reasons, then do it. Keep that taped in your home office somewhere and in plain sight, a continual reminder of why you made the crazy decision to be an Internet marketer.

Note that Berrig also emphasizes the importance of coachability, which is why I chose to spend an entire chapter on it. I like her use of the word "open" with the word "coachable." That is a great mental picture for how you need to be as you learn more of the business.

....
[7] Ibid.

Attitude

Finally, I very much appreciate her connection between a positive attitude and understanding what you do and do not have control over. Think through what this means for you in your enterprise. Can you absolutely control the number of views you get on your page and blog? No. You can do a lot to increase those numbers, but you can't ultimately control your progress.

Can you control whether or not a given client decides to do business with you? You can certainly do a lot to influence his/her decision, from being prepared in your presentation to figuring out the most persuasive way to bring them around to your point of view. In the end, however, the decision is the client's, and who knows how s/he thinks?

You cannot control such matters; you can only choose to maintain a positive attitude and press on. Consequently, to quote Berrig, "there will be no room for discouragement in your business". If you can answer with conviction the questions that she poses, you will be unbeatable as an Internet marketer. If you can tell someone quickly and succinctly why you got into the business, what you are doing to meet your goals and why you are confident in your direction, you will be a true force in the industry. There is plenty of room for more success stories, I assure you!

Lynn Brown also talks about the importance of a positive attitude, with this insight into the "nitty gritty" of Internet marketing:

> I can't state this enough: If you want to become a *successful online entrepreneur*, you need to embrace the power of a positive attitude.
>
> When I was building up my online business, there were so many obstacles and setbacks that made me want to crawl into bed and hide away for a few days. It seemed like I was taking one step forward, and fifty steps back. I felt like I always had something to worry about. Why wasn't my *website* ranking the way it should? Why isn't site traffic coming in? How can I find the time to work on my business when I barely have enough time to brush my teeth?
>
> But you know what kept me working right through these worries and concerns? My positive attitude. I just knew if I kept that smile on my face...that if I kept working and finding ways around my obstacles...that if I inherently believed it would all work out for me...I would become an online success.

Attitude

> A positive attitude isn't about being overly optimistic. It's about having the *confidence* to understand that your strength, integrity, and dedication is enough to power through any roadblock on the journey to online success.[8]

Please notice the distinction that Brown makes between having a positive attitude and being overly optimistic. Being overly optimistic can be very dangerous. You might think that you can be sloppy and inattentive to certain aspects of your business, but that you will still carve out a nice niche in the marketplace.

Having a positive attitude, however, sees reality and calls it for what it is, yet still anchors itself in a strong belief in self. It's believing in your "strength, integrity and dedication". It's not an either/or proposition: either you believe in yourself and maintain a good attitude or you work hard and have a negative attitude. Rather, it is a 'both' mind-set: I will work hard, but at the end of the day I will realize that I cannot control everything. I will maintain my positive attitude no matter how many setbacks I have in a given day. I will not lose faith in myself, and one day I will enjoy a piece of the pie.

Attitude is an important part of the Internet marketer's make-up, but it is not the only part of that make-up. You will need to draw on the other traits described in this book to put in the necessary work to earn a good living on the Web.

Maintaining a "Beginner's Mind"

Before I offer some closing thoughts on attitude, I want to offer one more ingredient to the mix of your attitude. I trust that you are not too overwhelmed by the number of elements that I have included as part of a winning attitude that will carry the day, no matter how grey it is.

I do not want to push any particular religion in this book; it is entirely beside the point, but I do want to share a helpful concept from Buddhism that could be of assistance as you formulate the proper attitude for achievement.

This concept is called "beginner's mind", and it means to approach any concept with an empty mind, as if you have much to learn. Internet marketer Vena Jensen Blitsch puts it this way:

---

[8] *http://learnit2earnitwithlynn.com/internet-marketing/online-basic-tips/the-importance-of-a-positive-attitude/#sthash.VRI7xmSw.dpuf*, retrieved 4.10.13.

Attitude

> When we believe we are an "expert" we think of ourselves as an "achiever" and we become over-confident. As a result, we experience a closed mind. In social media, as in life, there is always much to learn, always new understanding. When we approach social media marketing with an open mind, as if we are a blank slate, we maintain a willingness to learn and grow; we allow our stakeholders, teachers and others show us how to participate in this new way of doing business with a new perspective.[9]

This part of attitude overlaps a bit with my chapter on Coachability, obviously, but the melding of the different elements of this book is a beautiful, not an ugly, thing. The moment that we come to our work with a closed mind, as if we know it all, or certainly all that we need to know, we can find ourselves in trouble.

Our field is too dynamic, too fluid and too future-oriented to enable any of us to claim that we know all there is to know. The alternative, as offered by Blitsch, is to approach our work with a "beginner's mind". We come as a blank slate, as she says, and are teachable each day, guarding our humble attitude as we persevere to accomplish our goals.

Not only does this mind-set cause us to be humble and teachable, it will actually make us more flexible, which we always need to be in our industry. Blitsch explains:

> A beginner's mind causes us to break out of old habits, old ways of doing things. A beginner's mind opens us to concepts, thoughts, ideas and possibilities we couldn't imagine otherwise. When we have the attitude of a beginner's mind, we approach each day as if it is our first day learning new ways of interacting with others and the environment in which we find ourselves. Having a beginner's mind means we observe before charging ahead, ask questions when we aren't sure, and listen more than we talk.[10]

Keep a beginner's mind as part of your positive attitude and see if you break out of old habits that might be holding you back from even greater levels

---

[9] http://www.vibrantinternetmarketing.com/2012/04/04/the-right-attitude-for-social-media-marketing/, retrieved 4.10.13.

[10] Ibid.

Attitude

of accomplishment. Think of each day as an Internet marketer as your first day in the field, and be open to new ideas and possibilities. Picture your journey to being a credible Internet marketer as an adventure, not just a job or career. Prepare yourself for a future full of change as you start each day as if you know nothing, and are thus open to the twists and turns that Internet marketing will take. I will have more thoughts on the future of Internet marketing in my Conclusion chapter.

CHAPTER 6

COMMITMENT

Internet marketing is not a get-rich-quick scheme. Will you have the patience to weather ups and downs, good and bad, before you achieve the results you desire?

It's important to ask yourself this question before launching a career in Internet marketing or any other field – and to ignore anyone who tries to tell you that it will be easy and require little effort on your part.

Perhaps more than any other quality, commitment is crucial for anyone looking to build something of their lives. I didn't get the results I wanted right away. Most other success stories also included set-backs and failures before they reached the heights that they are known for. Just take a look around you at people whose career you admire or even famous business executives, from Bill Gates to Sir Richard Branson. Did they let failure deter them once they had decided to commit to an idea? I have found that even people with a career path that appears to have been smooth have gone through periods of back-breaking work and untold effort before striking it big.

Unfortunately, many people abandon their dreams all too quickly when they hit a stumbling block or an obstacle they failed to foresee or plan ahead for. I know it's easy to get discouraged when you put in the work but fail to see the results of your efforts. However, that is where the principle of commitment comes into play.

Take steps to build up your resolve before launching yourself into any field, especially Internet marketing. Remind yourself that it will take time to get the recognition and profitability you're working for, and that you'll need a passion for the job to guide you every step of the way.

When I pledged to be my own boss and to start building my career with little direction from anyone else, I didn't expect that it would always be a smooth and easy ride – and it hasn't been. You too must recognize that there will be bumps in the road and challenges you'll have to confront. Are you willing to commit yourself to your start-up during times of hardship as well as in times of plenty? I, for one, am glad I took the chance, backed it up with hard work and wasn't deterred by difficult tasks or results that were slow in coming.

Developing a commitment to success is easier said than done, however. As an Internet marketer, it may be easy to fall prey to the misguided idea that the money will start rolling in right away. In fact, if you are married to the notion that you'll be flush with cash while sitting on your couch and only working an hour a day, you'll end up wasting money in start-up costs because you won't stick with your plan long enough to get a return on your investment.

Caution: Commitment Absolutely Necessary to Success

Instead, as with any business, you will need to realize that you'll have to make sacrifices at the beginning and that it may take some time before your efforts yield any results. One of the top traits of Internet marketers is a commitment to success.[1] Especially in the beginning, you'll need to pledge yourself to your goal in order to get through the initial growing pains. This commitment has continued to guide me, both through my daily routine and as a long-term principle.

But just how do you give a commitment to a concept?

How to Build Your Commitment

You can strengthen your determination and resolve by following these steps, taken from other examples of highly successful Internet marketers who put them into practice every day.

1. Don't be afraid of failure!

There's no question that the idea of failure is frightening to many people. For some, this fear of failure can actually become paralysing and keep them from pursuing their dreams.

Instead of visualizing the freedom in being self-employed, these people stay in corporate jobs and cubicles because the idea of failure is so

---

[1] *http://birdherd.com/the-10-essential-qualities-of-a-successful-internet-marketer/* Retrieved 27.9.13

crippling as to prevent them from charting their own course. That's why you'll find that many successful self-employed people are immune to the fear of failure.[2]

The concept of failure in our culture is often overwhelmingly negative. Culturally, failing at something is a sign of a person who is uneducated, who lacks ambition or who is unrealistic in their goals. People who are scared of failure worry endlessly about what they'd say to friends and family members, or how they would be perceived by others if they took a chance and didn't succeed right away.

However, successful self-employed people know that failure isn't always a bad thing. In fact, it is often the learning experience that will become the underlying reason for future successful endeavours.

Committing myself to Internet marketing did not require me to abandon all sense of reality. Instead, I asked myself and answered honestly, "What if I fail?"

This question has both financial and emotional implications. It has affected everything from how much money and resources I decided to invest at the start, knowing that they might be wasted, to my self-esteem, or how I would think of myself if I didn't achieve my goals.

Failure is a possibility with any effort, whether due to unforeseen circumstances or a flawed plan. As a self-starter, I couldn't allow it to affect my sense of self or emotional wellbeing. I knew it was worth more to me to try it out than to wonder "What if?" for the rest of my life.

You will also have to be willing to take the plunge, all the while knowing that it might not work out – but that you'll be the better person for having tried.

However, if you're the type of person who can't handle failure and is more concerned about how others perceive you, this may not be the career for you. Remember that Internet marketing is not a safe bet; like any other career, it will take self-discipline, planning, proper management and creative thinking to blossom.

Even after you've launched your Internet marketing plan, this nagging fear of failure that is so culturally prevalent can lead to inaction. With the countless decisions you'll be facing daily as your own boss, hesitation

---

[2] *http://www.helium.com/items/748091-personality-traits-necessary-for-success-in-self-employment* Retrieved 27.9.13

Commitment

prompted by fear of saying or doing the wrong thing will slow down your momentum. Consider this advice, courtesy of *Entrepreneur* magazine's interviews, uncovering the secrets of successful marketers:

> Take action without hesitation. I trust my gut on the right thing to do when faced with any business decision, and I don't procrastinate when I know what I need to do. Without action, results can't manifest, and I've found that many people know what they need to do, but have trouble taking action on it. If you can overcome your hesitations and excuses, you'll find that you can be much more productive.
> - Jayson DeMers, *AudienceBloom*[3]

Instead of coming up with all the reasons you can to avoid launching your own business or to keep yourself from putting in the time and resources, take the leap into the world of the self-employed. While failure is a possibility, so are unprecedented levels of success.

Image credit: <a href='http://www.123rf.com/photo_18283501_powerful-solutions-with-a-businessman-levitating-above-a-maze-or-labyrinth-as-a-business-concept-of-.html'>lightwise / 123RF Stock Photo</a>

---

[3] *http://www.entrepreneur.com/article/228059#ixzz2f49wLitY* Retrieved 27.9.13.

Commitment

2. Develop your discipline.

Making a commitment to something involves resisting temptations that can lead you astray. Discipline is a fundamental component of commitment to a business, an idea, even a spouse.

One good example that proves the correlation between discipline and commitment is the classic New Year's resolution to get in shape. I could declare my commitment to being healthy all I want, but it would be a shallow promise if I didn't pair it with discipline, such as going to the gym or resisting foods that are bad for me.

Another example could be a musician's commitment to becoming a virtuoso on a particular instrument. What kind of commitment would it be without the discipline of practising every day?

As an Internet marketer, both discipline and commitment are required. In my daily routine, these principles guide me when it comes to resisting what sounds like better offers or even if I simply don't feel like working very hard on a given day.

Once you decide on the path of Internet marketing, you will also have to stick with it if you want to have a chance of succeeding – and that will involve copious amounts of discipline, especially during the initial growth phase of your business when you will need to devote yourself to your idea like no other.

Many people want to become a success in online fields such as Internet marketing, but they won't go very far without both commitment and discipline.[4]

Discipline will be key, not just to staying committed to your path, but also as a crucial factor in your success. It will come into play in all aspects of your chosen career, from time management to organization.

I have come across too many people who are sold on a rosy idea of working from home, but who don't actually have the drive required to start or run an online business. They quickly discover that it isn't all about spending more time with the family or having the freedom to do what they want each day. In fact, at the start, having free time is often out of the question.

Some tips I have learned for helping to establish one's commitment include:

---

[4] *http://www.metacafe.com/watch/3367354/why_discipline_commitment_are_so_important_in_business/* Retrieved 1.10.13

Commitment

Image credit: <a href='http://www.123rf.com/photo_22482826_scruffy-looking-unemployed-man-sitting-home-in-his-bathrobe-using-his-tablet-pc.html'>lisafx / 123RF Stock Photo</a>

- Don't work in pyjamas: This is a classic stereotype associated with the self-employed. While I don't have to follow a strict office dress code, I know that professionalism is what my clients expect. While comfort helps, don't abandon all practices of the office world, such as getting up and getting ready for the day.
- Create a separate work area: Setting up a home office or a quiet place where you are not disturbed allows you to accomplish the goals and tasks you set out for yourself each day. Instead of working from the kitchen table or curled up in bed, going to your home office will prepare you mentally for the day ahead. Many experts agree that establishing a work area helps self-employed people devote themselves to their career.[5] It also sends a signal to friends who may wish to drop in or family members who are also at home that you are working even though you're at home.
- Set work hours: As an online business owner, your clients will expect you to accomplish certain things by a certain time. That's why having established office hours when you will be available is important. This goes against the idea that most people have of working from home, but it helps you to stay on task. Although setting your own schedule is one of the benefits of being

---

[5] http://www.eliteemployees.com/methods-to-increase-your-commitment-and-discipline-in-your-home-business/ Retrieved 1.10.13

Commitment

self-employed, it doesn't mean you should completely disregard all notion of office hours. Create a schedule that works for you and stick to it.[6]

3. Be patient!

Perhaps the most important trait you'll need in Internet marketing is patience. Your business will grow over time and you probably won't see the results right away – but if you become impatient and stop putting in the time, you won't get the payout.

To those looking from the outside in, it may be difficult to see why a self-employed person is putting in so many work hours for little return in the initial stages of launching their own career. But a successful self-employed Internet marketer will know that these efforts will pay for themselves over and over again. [7]

When I first got started, I expected there to be a learning curve. Although I had a rudimentary knowledge of Internet marketing practices, I wasn't an expert in all of the factors that go into it. It takes effort to drive website traffic and attract attention from customers – gone are the days when Internet marketers could take it easy and let clients come to them.

Just a few examples of practices Internet marketers will need to master include search engine optimization, link exchanges, online advertising practices and affiliate programmes.[8] All of these efforts will also require constant monitoring to see if they should be amended or scrapped altogether if they aren't working.

In the initial stages, I also needed to remind myself that I had to have realistic expectations of how long it would take before I could achieve visibility in a crowded marketplace. It's old news that search engines are changing their algorithms all the time to prevent black hat Internet marketing practices, such as spamming or keyword stuffing. For the legitimate Internet marketer, that also means a lot of follow-up will be required after launching any particular effort, and results may be subject to change.

---

[6] Ibid.

[7] *http://www.thinkbigmagazine.com/business/254-successfully-self-employed* Retrieved 27.9.13

[8] *http://www.smallbizsmartmarketing.com/articles/article_patience.htm* Retrieved 2.10.13

Commitment

I learned that it took time to find the customers I was looking for. Patience is required before Internet marketers achieve their target audience.In addition, studies have shown that potential customers need to get familiar with what you're selling before they're inclined to make a purchase and may need to encounter your methods between seven and twelve times before they're ready to commit.[9]

Researching the methods you want to use and then monitoring those methods will require patience. I have also found that some strategies yield unexpected results, which require me to update my original plan or move forward in an entirely new direction. As an Internet marketer, I am constantly making slight changes to existing strategies as I monitor them in order to achieve the results, audience and profits that I am looking for.

Don't waste all your energy looking for short-cuts, as true expertise is far more valuable – and profitable. Besides, search engine algorithms have become sophisticated enough to detect efforts at gaming the system, which means the relentless pursuit of short-cuts will be in vain.

I have also found that one of the many highlights of Internet marketing is ongoing learning. As new technologies emerge and become popular, I have to be ahead of the curve by staying on top of trends. Internet marketing is often thought of as a sort of frontier, with many in the field eager to master the latest advances. Instead of letting this be a source of frustration, I have cultivated patience when it comes to getting familiar with the latest techniques. It's a habit that other successful online entrepreneurs also share.[10]

Rather than constantly looking for the easy way out, Internet marketers look at challenges as opportunities for growth. They remind themselves that all difficulties can be overcome with the right combination of perseverance, patience and grit.[11]

4. Prioritize.

Internet marketers are responsible for their own future. That's why it is all too easy for them to get caught up in the minutiae of their daily tasks, and lose sight of their long-term goals.

---

[9] *http://realtytimes.com/todaysheadlines1/item/1483-20111027_patience* Retrieved 2.10.13

[10] *http://lucybieri.com/online-marketing-patience-necessary-survive* Retrieved 2.10.13

[11] *http://www.helium.com/items/748091-personality-traits-necessary-for-success-in-self-employment* Retrieved 3.10.13

Commitment

Self-employed business owners, such as Internet marketers, are often the only ones responsible for every aspect of their livelihood. There is no one else to field questions from clients and make the sale or to do the grunt work, such as answering phone calls and emails, tracking expenses, payroll and hours. Then there's the side of work necessary to keep growing, such as taking the time to stay current on technological trends or networking at industry events or in forums. Far from the idea most people have of the self-employed, an Internet marketer can often put in more hours than an office worker – especially at the start!

Although multi-tasking is indeed crucial, it is also important not to lose sight of priorities. Every business success knows their strengths and weaknesses. They know how much time to dedicate to a particular task and when their efforts are futile. They know when it's time to outsource and when to handle it themselves.[12]

Initially for Internet marketers, delegating tasks to others may not be an option. But when it comes to managing their time wisely to handle competing obligations, such as traffic building versus implementing new techniques, that can certainly be managed for maximum effectiveness and returns.

There's no question that there is a mountain of advice out there for Internet marketers regarding what techniques they should be using. If the entrepreneur just starting out decides, unwisely, to pursue all of these options, with little regard to what they already bring to the table or which offers better returns, they will quickly become frazzled and unfocused, lose sight of their goals and may burn out too quickly.[13]

An easy way for Internet marketers to prioritize, when they're starting to feel overwhelmed, is to focus on the bottom line.

That means not wasting time on tasks that don't contribute to the growth of your business or putting your fingers in too many pots – PPC, banner advertising, search engine optimization or social media – that simply aren't generating profits.

Here is some tried-and-tested advice from experienced Internet marketers that can help you determine if you are prioritizing effectively:

---

[12] *http://www.entrepreneur.com/article/200730#ixzz2f4BulUgC* Retrieved 3.10.13

[13] *http://www.palmerwebmarketing.com/blog/a-paradox-of-choice-prioritizing-web-marketing-tactics/* Retrieved 3.10.13

Commitment

- **Come up with a strategy before deciding on a tactic:** Who are you trying to reach? By establishing your end game before getting started, you'll be less likely to lose sight of your goals. For many Internet marketers, this will be an intimate portrait of the audience they're going for. Are they young, old, professionals, artists or stay-at-home moms? This in turn will guide you when it comes to choosing the tactics to use to reach them among the many options available. For example, using social media to reach a younger, more connected audience would be smarter than trying to reach senior citizens with the same method. Each time you decide to launch a new initiative or try the latest new technique, ask yourself if it pairs well with your strategy before investing too much time or money.
- **Keep track of results:** Although it's not always easy to see the fruit of your labour as an Internet marketer, you should be quantifying your efforts and focusing on the bottom line. If something isn't working, scrap it quickly at a low cost before throwing more time or money at the problem. Gauge which of your marketing tactics are performing well, and devote more of your time to improving those already positive results. It's far more effective to invest more effort into a marketing strategy that is working for you, rather than attempt to bring a poorly performing strategy up to par.[14]
- **Stay up to speed with the competition**: If other peers in the field are all jumping on board with a new marketing technique or strategy, chances are you should be, too. It isn't necessary to be the most innovative Internet marketer in the field, but it is important to stay current – even if you're not the first. Keep in mind the previous two rules regarding how much time, money or effort you should be investing in relation to the returns you can expect. But don't neglect keeping tabs on the competitors or Internet marketers you admire. Internet marketers never really know how long a proven strategy will continue to generate results. That's why keeping up with the latest up-and-coming strategies is important for a healthy business in the long-term.

Whether you're a fledgling Internet marketer or an established one, having the right priorities will help you shoot to the top before flaming out. If you're starting to feel burdened by too many tasks or struggling to remember why you started out in this field in the first place, it's helpful to remember that it's happened to the best of them. Instead of dreaming about quitting and going back to the conventional workforce where there's always someone to tell you what to do, take a moment to refresh your commitment to your online business by prioritizing your tasks with an eye on the results. Then, schedule your time to allow more effort to go into the high-performing strategies. Cut yourself some slack if you find

---

[14] Ibid.

Commitment

that you're simply not good at a certain task, by outsourcing or dropping it from your overall plan.

5. Never stop learning.

After making any type of commitment, it's important to keep the romance alive from time to time. Sometimes we forget why we made the choices we made, as the daily grind and competing interests drain our energy and time. When we lose sight of the core of our commitment, it can be difficult to stay focused. Suddenly, every obstacle seems like the end.

In a romantic partnership, it's well-established advice that keeping things fresh helps the commitment last. A surprise date night, travelling to a new place together or simply taking the time to talk with each other over a cup of coffee can be the bright spot in a dreary day and help a couple keep going.

Of course, I'm not writing this book to tell you the secrets to a lasting marriage. But I've found that this analogy works when it comes to describing the commitment you'll need to succeed in Internet marketing as well. For the Internet marketer, keeping the torch lit in a crowded and competitive field won't involve buying a sweetheart a gift or some concert tickets to see a favourite band, but successful online entrepreneurs remind themselves why they do what they do by constantly learning, refreshing and adding to their skills.[15]

The field of Internet marketing is never static. The techniques of yesterday no longer apply to today, and today's popular methods may not work tomorrow. However, too many Internet marketers rely heavily on practices they picked up too long ago. Though these online strategies may be working – for now – keeping up-to-date will ensure that you won't wake up one day with an outdated image and skills set. Technology can be fleeting, so the "never stop learning" mantra doesn't mean that all Internet marketers should hop on the bandwagon just because their competitors are doing it. But, even if you decide not to implement one strategy or another, being aware of the trends and how effective they are will mean that you won't get left in the dust.[16]

Keeping up with the shifting landscape of Internet marketing could end up being a full-time job in itself, of course. Since most Internet marketers

---

[15] *http://www.thunderseo.com/blog/online-marketing-resources/* Retrieved 3.10.13

[16] *http://info.tmrdirect.com/bid/118174/Back-To-School-For-Marketers-Why-Learning-Should-Never-Stop* Retrieved 3.10.13

Commitment

are already drawn to the field because they're innovative, forward-thinking people, it's important to remember that growing your home business is still the bottom line.

But the commitment to constant learning doesn't have to be a time-eater either. One simple way that Internet marketers can make sure they're not missing out on the Next Big Thing is to subscribe to an Internet marketing forum, industry newsletter or blog. Taking a little time over a cup of coffee in the morning to browse the headlines is a simple way to stay up to date. It can also be a source of excitement and motivation that will help you to remember why you got into the industry, and to stay on task throughout the day.

Another way Internet marketers can continue to keep learning is by attending conferences. These venues offer a two-for-one benefit: the chance to dissect the latest trends, and network with potential colleagues or clients at the same time.[17]

Image credit: <a href='http://www.123rf.com/photo_18736285_audience-listening-to-presentation-at-conference.html'>stockbroker / 123RF Stock Photo</a>

Constant learning isn't just a commitment to keeping up with trends and technology, though. It also involves an introspective look at what is

---

[17] http://www.iacquire.com/blog/2013-online-marketing-conferences-events/ Retrieved 3.10.13

Commitment

working and what's not when it comes to a home business.[18] You already know that monitoring the results of your efforts as an Internet marketer will be a fundamental part of any strategy – you have to know what is working and what isn't, if you want to be successful. The same goes for your errors. Don't ignore your mistakes, or you won't learn anything from them. Instead, evaluate why you made a wrong move to avoid falling into a negative pattern.

In my career, the directive for constant education means evaluating my mistakes and learning from them in addition to finding new marketing methods and ways to communicate. Evaluating my errors has helped my business blossom in new ways I never thought possible.

No one knows all there is to know about Internet marketing. That's why even so-called experts in the field are always looking to improve.[19]

---

[18] *http://themyndset.com/2012/01/the-future-of-learning-how-should-your-company-adapt-and-encourage-constant-learning/* Retrieved 3.10.13

[19] *https://blog.viralgains.com/2013/07/easy-to-understand-tips-marketing-internet/* Retrieved 3.10.13

CHAPTER 7

CONCLUSION: THE FUTURE OF INTERNET MARKETING

I hope that this book has been helpful to you. It would be amiss to end this book without a look at the future of Internet marketing. No matter what I predict here, please keep in mind that the tenets of the first six chapters remain unchanged. The traits that I have covered will hold true no matter

Image credit: <a href='http://www.123rf.com/photo_20993983_smart-phone-with-cloud-of-application-icons-in-consumer-hand.html'>shutter999 / 123RF Stock Photo</a>

Conclusion: The Future Of Internet Marketing

how the future unfolds. That makes this book, in a sense, timeless, and a worthy investment of your energy and money.

I have my own thoughts on where our industry is going, some fairly standard, some not so commonplace. You are free to disagree with my ideas.

I share all of these having done a fair amount of research on the topic, as well as reflecting on trends that I have noticed in my personal work. I trust that you will keep the teachable attitude that I have discussed at length within this book. If I can do anything to help you prepare for what is around the corner in Internet marketing, I want to do that.

Here, then, are my 10 trends to look for in the future of Internet marketing:

1. Our entire domain of business will continue to be shaped by the final destinations of our marketing. In other words, think mobile and global. All of our marketing must keep the continuing, explosive growth of worldwide cell phone and tablet usage in mind. More than ever, people are looking at their phone screens and tablets as they shop and are exposed to our marketing and this will continue to grow in the future. As a result, you need to plan accordingly in your strategies. Whatever content you hope to deliver to the customer, it must look great on a cell phone screen and tablet. Not only that, but many will soon be looking at even tinier screens — on their watch faces. This will also shape our specialty.

2. Twitter will continue to edge up to Facebook's level, and Pinterest will continue to challenge Twitter. Twitter is, in some ways, the new Facebook, and Pinterest is the new Twitter. What will follow Pinterest? Keep your eyes open. One thing is for sure: social media will not stay static. Look for a site that can deliver video cheaply and quickly. Perhaps Vine will be the Next Big Thing.

3. Due to the changing patterns discussed above in point 2, you will need to work on your photo and video editing skills. The triumph of the image over long text will not be reversed. The next conquest will be the video over the photo. Prepare accordingly.

4. The world will get even flatter, which means that customer input will become more widespread, and customer opinion will be more highly valued than ever. The evolution away from a top-down system will continue, even if governments do not catch on! On the Net, the order of people will continue

Conclusion: The Future Of Internet Marketing

to flatten, meaning that people will trust company-produced content less and customer reviews and social content more. That's bad news for some who will want to market through us. The Internet marketer who can capture this strong trend by the tail will be way ahead of the game. Along with this flatter world will be even more interaction between customers and vendors. Think long and hard about how you can facilitate that in your marketing. This will give you an edge with any client.

5. As analytics expertise continues to become more available, our clients will demand more. There will be less haziness over whether a given campaign was "successful". More numbers than ever will be available to prove or disprove that notion. This means that we will all have to up our game and not hide anything from our clients. We should actually beat them to the punch by making the most relevant numbers easily accessible to them. There will be less deception over the merits of given marketing campaigns. It will be "statistics run amok", for better or for worse.

6. Authors of content will be more important than websites. New forms of ranking favour authors who are credible and have a wide following. If you want to be one of those authors, you will need to study hard and become an expert in some slice of the field. If you want to sell a product, try to find authors who are respected and followed.

7. SEO will diminish as community-building rises. I believe that there will be less emphasis on technique in SEO than on branding and constructing strong connections between audiences and products. Across the board, people who make their living on the Net are calling for greater transparency and more vivid humanity in marketing. Think more art than science on this one. That will call for greater creativity from all of us. It will be harder than ever to game the system, and black hat marketers will have a more difficult time making a living, which is good for all of us.

8. Many experts are saying that content marketing will continue to grow, at the expense of ads. The idea is that people are now very at home on the Web, and they will insist on verifiable sources of information to make their choices. They will want solid research and trustworthy reviews to guide their choices, not flashy advertisements and phoney reviews.

9. The tools that we use to build our business will become cheaper and better. This happens in any technological industry, of which we are one. This is great news for those of you who are considering a start-up in the near future. You can jump into the fray for less money than ever.

Conclusion: The Future Of Internet Marketing

10. Expensive e-books and DVD training courses are on the way out. Content will have to be backed up with consulting and high value seminars. Many marketers are now giving away e-books for free and putting content on YouTube and other sites.

To end on an encouraging note, many Internet marketers think that the next year or two will be particularly revelatory for businesses. We have all been waiting for the time when every businessperson in the world understands that if they are not on the Net, they are leaving money on the table. Given the continual flow of businesses to the Web, this day may be fast approaching.

This means that there will be more business for all of us and more opportunity for those who want to jump on board, work hard and make a go of it.

My advice? Make sure that you have a deep desire to succeed. Check your motivation, verify that it comes from within, and have several sources to feed it continually. Don't forget to plan carefully before diving into these sometimes-treacherous waters. As you do plan, keep a coachable, learner attitude that lasts a lifetime. Finally, maintain a positive, can-do, indomitable attitude while you stick with your commitment to soldier on no matter what obstacles present themselves.

Remember: many people work in dying industries. Their futures are very uncertain. But we do not. We work in a thriving industry that is welcoming new players every day. There is money to be made on the Web. I hope that this book will help you to make some of it.

Finally, be generous with your charitable offerings. In the online world of plenty, giving is as rewarding and enjoyable as making money on the Web.

The proceeds of this book will go to the Patrick Headley charity fund, for more details go to www.patrickheadley.com.